LEGEI

AND

REBELS

OF THE FOOTBALL WORLD

NORM PARKIN

A refreshing insight to the football world, with
forthcoming interviews, funny stories, and
opinions about the past, present and future of
the "beautiful game".

i

First Published in 2014 by Norman Parkin.
Written by Norman Parkin.
Editing by Anne Grange at
Wild Rosemary Writing Services.
Copyright © Norman Parkin 2014

The proceeds from this book will be donated to
the Philippines Typhoon relief fund: the
*International One Way Outreach Ministry
Permeating Bantayan Island, Tacloban & Leyte
areas Disaster Relief*, and the *Rehabilitation
Committee (DRRC) Ministry Cosmopolitan
Church Permeating Bohol and Leyte Areas.*
http://thecosmopolitanchurch.org/

ISBN: 978-1-326-05806-7

CONTENTS

Introduction   Page 1

Foreword by Leo Jensen   Page 4

Acknowledgements   Page 9

Chapter 1: The Philippine Connection Page 12

Chapter 2 Ron Atkinson   Page 28

Chapter 3 Mel Sterland   Page 42

Chapter 4 Eddie Gray   Page 52

Chapter 5 Ken Wagstaff   Page 62

Chapter 6 Harry Gregg   Page 68

Chapter 7 Carlton Palmer   Page 82

Chapter 8 Stanley Matthews   Page 90

Chapter 9 Don Rogers   Page 102

Chapter 10 Archie Gemmill   Page 112

Chapter 11 Neil Warnock   Page 121

Chapter 12 David Hirst   Page 142

Chapter 13 Frank Worthington Page 153

Chapter 14 Keith Hackett   Page 163

Chapter 15 Tom Finney   Page 175

Chapter 16   David Layne   Page 182

Chapter 17   Kenny Burns   Page 187

Chapter 18   Jimmy Greaves   Page 201

Chapter 19   Peter Lorimer   Page 208

Chapter 20   Malcolm Macdonald   Page 217

Chapter 21   Chris Waddle   Page 232

Chapter 22   Philip Scorthorne   Page 246

Chapter 23   Jürgen Grabowski   Page 257

Chapter 24   Parkin's Observations   Page 269

INTRODUCTION

In the past, lots of my friends have often told me that I should write a book about my exploits.

I've led an action-packed life, living in and visiting many different places around the world.

A few years ago, I did think about writing my life story once or twice, but I never got it off the ground.

To be honest, I find it much more interesting to write about other people. Then I came up with this idea, and here you have it!

It's true that I have led a very colourful life – more than most, but I always think that people don't want to know about certain aspects of your life. I find the idea of writing a book about myself and everything that I have done a little self-indulgent.

In fact, one of the characters in this book, David Hirst, told me that he did not want to write his autobiography, because he felt that other people would suffer from the content of his stories.

He didn't like the way that some ex-players have written their autobiographies and have included scandalous stories that David knows for a fact aren't true, just to sell more books!

This book is different. I wrote it because I wanted to celebrate the great football legends and characters. Most of the characters in the book had special qualities or talents which touched me, and inspired me in my own football career.

It really was great fun to organize the interviews and to have the chance to chat to these football giants from the past.

Some of the tales they told were outrageous to say the least, whilst others just didn't want to share too much about certain parts of their own football history.

The characters in this book were as different as "chalk and cheese" to interview, some of them outrageous extroverts, and some of them enjoying a quiet retirement away from the public eye.

You must remember that each ex-footballer told me their own opinions, which do not always reflect my own!

I'm sure that every football fan reading this book will find players they worshipped back in their day, from the fifties to the nineties.

I hope you enjoy reading the book as much as I did writing it!

Norman Parkin

Leeds step in to make 'twin' capture

LEEDS UNITED, famous throughout the game for their schoolboy scoops, have made a successful "twin" assault in Sheffield.

Elland Road bound are twin brothers, Maurice and Norman Parkin, having signed schoolboy amateur forms.

Both attend Jordanthorpe Secondary and will join Don Revie's camp as apprentice professionals on leaving school.

The long arm of the Leeds scouting system spotted the brothers even before they came up for Sheffield Boys' team trials in the last few weeks.

Both were in the successful Jordanthorpe side of last season, Maurice being captain and top scorer from the inside right position.

Leeds United - bound twin brothers, Norman (left) a Maurice doing a bit of "homework" on their boots

★ Quick move

Leeds moved in quickly and following talks with the boys' parents, Mr. and Mrs. Herbert Parkin, the twin signing was completed.

Maurice has now gone overboard for the Leeds way of life.

So much so that he has switched position to right half in order to style himself on his Leeds favourite, Billy Bremner!

Norman is a very strong type of defender and plays full back or centre half.

On the Leeds signing, Mr. Parkin, a grinder, said from his home at Spring Close Dell, Gleadless Valley, Sheffield:

"The directors of the club invited us over to Elland Road to see for ourselves the set-up for their apprentice professionals.

★ Impressed

"We were very impressed and it will be up to the boys to make the best of the chance."

Wasn't he sorry that a Sheffield club hadn't stepped in first?

I'm not really football minded myself.

How it all began: My brother Maurice and I were signed to Leeds United as fourteen-year-old schoolboys in 1964.

As you can tell, we've treasured the Sheffield Star newspaper cutting from that day.

FOREWORD – BY LEO JENSEN

I first met Norman in Glossop, a small Pennine town, not too far from where I live.

Norman has had quite a globetrotting life with football.

He and his brother Maurice were spotted at school by a Leeds United scout, and were enrolled on a coaching program.

Soon afterwards, the Leeds manager at that time, Don Revie, moved in and signed both of them to the club at the age of fourteen.

Norman wasn't retained by Leeds, and so moved onto Chesterfield, where he befriended the now well-known Neil Warnock.

At the age of twenty, Norman decided to play abroad, and later to coach abroad too, starting in Australia, where he played for Greek team Pan Hellenic for three years, and then he moved on to Malta, Hong Kong, Brazil, America, the Philippines, and then back to England.

In some countries he played football, and in others, he concentrated on coaching.

In Malta, he played in the European Cup for Sliema Wanderers, against the mighty German team Eintracht Frankfurt, and even exchanged shirts with German International World Cup winner Jürgen Grabowski.

While living in Malta, Norman had the great pleasure of meeting the late, great Sir Stanley Matthews.

Sir Stanley kindly invited Norman for lunch and chatted to him for hours about his past football days. Decades later, Norman still really cherishes his meeting with Sir Stan.

Norman also coached voluntarily in Rio, Brazil, back in the 80s. He taught in the so-called "Favelas", the really poor area of Rio, shanty houses with tin roofs, perched on the hillside.

This district was very dangerous for outsiders unless they were accompanied by some of the locals who lived there, or someone who was well-known in the area. Typically, Norman took it all in his stride.

With a Brazilian fan inside the Maracanã Stadium in Rio, 1986.

Norman played for numerous semi-professional teams, before finally hanging his boots up after his time in Texas, USA, playing with the Houston Dynamos and Houston Express (indoor league).

Norm was in good company: the great England and Leicester City player Keith Weller finished his playing career in Houston too.

Incidentally, Keith Weller was made famous by being the first player on British TV to wear a pair of tights during a game on a freezing cold day. Keith was a fine player; and he sadly died in 2004.

Norman also worked for a short time for B.B.C. Radio Sheffield, reporting on football matches.

He has also written reports and essays on Philippine football for the Philippine Football Federation.

Norman worked closely with the Federation's President, Mari Martinez. They were good friends and colleagues. When Mari Martinez passed away through illness in 2013, it was a sad day for Philippine football.

Norman has been coaching in The Philippines for over thirteen years. He's worked on and off at various levels, including a short spell with top college team De La Salle.

He has also helped to develop the "Grass Roots" football programme, put together in 2001 by Philippine Football

Federation President Johnny Romualdez and German football ambassador, Bernd Fischer.

Norman has also travelled around the Philippine provinces as a football coach. In Baguio, he met Leo Arnaiz, a well-respected football coach who teaches football to homeless street kids. Norman helps out whenever he is over there.

The street kids' programme is organised by a wonderful lady, Ruth Callanta. It's taking off in a big way – as the kids aren't just building up their football skills, but get an education and are developing their characters too.

Norm coaches as a freelancer with other teams too, so he hasn't slowed down at all over the years.

Year after year, Norm sees a vast improvement in Philippine football. He remembers a time when you had no chance of buying an English Premier League team shirt anywhere in the country, not even in the markets of the capital, Manila.

Now you can see why Norman has written this book and has dedicated it to all the victims of typhoon Yolanda in the Philippines. I hope it will help in some small way.

Norman definitely has an affinity with the Filipino people and their country. It is easy to see why he has put this project together and why he has spent so much time and effort in doing it.

I truly hope that this book is a great success, not only for my friend and colleague, but for the sake of the Philippine people who were the victims of this terrible catastrophe.

Leo Jensen
Philippine United F.C. founder, colleague and friend.

Coaching in Laguna, Philippines in 2013.

ACKNOWLEDGEMENTS

I really enjoyed finding these characters one by one, and it was great fun interviewing them.

To be honest, it was more like a football 'get together'. Most of the time in the interviews was spent laughing at old stories: some of them from the players, and also from my own experiences.

At the end of every interview, my friend and assistant coach Steve Conroy, took photographs for posterity, and I'd like to thank him for his ongoing support of my project.

I truly want to thank every one of my interviewees from the bottom of my heart, firstly for agreeing to do the interviews and photographs, and secondly, for making this book a total pleasure to write from beginning to end.

Thanks must also go to Anne Grange of Wild Rosemary Writing Services, who has edited and formatted the book. and Damian Tynan, who has also helped with the writing.

Some of the characters in the book were larger than life whilst some were a little bit inhibited in their interviews, but I can honestly say that every person in this book contributed something that helped to build the book's contents, with facts and figures, and certainly lots of laughter from old footballing stories.

I thank every last one of you, from Malcolm Macdonald to my old dear mate Phil Scorthorne.

The pleasure was all mine. It was fully worth all the hard work and travelling that we did to accomplish the finished article.

The inspiration for writing and putting this book together came to me in a simple vision. The thought of writing a book about footballing legends just got stuck in the back of my head until I decided to go with it and do it.

Mary Shelley had a vision in her dream about 'Frankenstein' and so she put it into words - and the rest is history.

There was a limit to the ex-footballers that I could include in my book, but there were some that I really wanted to interview that I could not manage to contact.

Or sadly, they are simply not with us anymore.

Some late, great players do get a mention in my book. I actually met Sir Stanley Matthews before he passed away, which was a great privilege.

I was due to interview Sir Tom Finney, only a few weeks before he died, so I gave him a chapter in his memory.

They were not only two of my own favourite players, but they were loved and respected by almost everyone.

I would have also loved to have interviewed ex-players and managers such as Bill Shankly, Billy Bremner, George Best, and the charismatic Brian Clough.

My next project may be about football heroes from foreign shores. Now wouldn't that be interesting?

Once again, I would like to thank everyone who has helped me to put this book together. It was well worth it.

Norm Parkin, Author.

Me in action in the early 80s!

CHAPTER ONE
THE PHILIPPINE CONNECTION

It was November the 8th 2013. My flight from Manchester was about to land in Manila, the capital of the Philippines, a destination I'd travelled to so many times before.

The aeroplane's captain announced over the loud speakers that the weather was very bad, and that special warnings had been issued all over the Philippines.

The plane was rather shaky, to say the least, and a few of the passengers were starting to panic, but after circling the airport a few times, we managed to land without any problems.

Tacloban: the storm surge slams a ship into houses.

What was to follow that day was horrendous, with devastating results for the population.

Over sixteen million people were badly affected by Typhoon Yolanda. It was like no other typhoon.

If you frequent the Philippines regularly, as I do, then you will know that the country is frequently hit by natural disasters. I have been a first-hand witness of more than my fair share of disaster stories.

On my very first visit a few years ago, there were very heavy floods in the Quezon City area, just outside Manila.

About ninety people lost their lives in the flooding, mainly because the banks of the river gave way and the poor people who live near the river bank got washed away.

A few years later, my friend Steve and I were staying in on the tenth floor of a Manila hotel.

One morning, Steve looked at me and said: 'Norm, look at that mirror on the wall."

I saw that the mirror was wobbling profusely, so we ran to the door. Everyone on our floor was panicking. We started running down the stairs. We got out okay but the panic was frightening.

It was only a mild earth tremor, but in the earthquake zone, every warning sign is taken seriously.

The best was yet to come.

Steve and I were football coaching for the ex-Philippine Football Federation President, Mr Mari Martinez.

We were working at a school in a town called Legaspi. Believe it or not, but the beautiful volcano in the background, Mount Mayon, started to erupt, and it gradually got worse, hour by hour.

Mount Mayon erupts, 19 August 2006.

The eruption continued while we were still coaching. Later that afternoon, the police came and told us all that we had to evacuate the school.

We must have only been half a mile away from the volcano and we could see the lava flow coming down the side of the mountain. The pictures that I took on that day are hanging on my wall at home.

I suppose I could also mention the time we all went out, celebrating our final day in the Philippines. We were drinking in a nightclub in Manila when we heard a loud bang. We all ran outside and were later told that a bomb had gone off in a bus, only five minutes from our night club.

While I was living "over the water" in the USA, in Houston, Texas, I experienced two hurricanes, a tornado and a horrendous flood, so you can see that I am definitely a bad-luck charm concerning disaster stories.

Yes, when Norm Parkin is in the Philippines (or the USA) there is never a dull moment.

Then to put the icing on the cake, I arrived on 8 November 2013, when the biggest typhoon in the Philippines' history hit the province of Leyte, completely destroying the town of Tacloban, with almost six thousand people dead and about four thousand people missing.

People were screaming and panicking everywhere we went. It was sheer pandemonium. Typhoon Yolanda was on the news twenty-four hours a day. Groups were organised to search for survivors, and there was total panic all over the city. It was like nothing I had ever seen before.

There were people staying in our hotel whose family members had gone missing, and they couldn't get in touch with anyone at all who might know what was going on.

It really was an eye-opener, especially when reality hit the people whose loved ones were missing.

Typhoon Yolanda: showing the vast scale of the damage.

This was the worst disaster that I have ever experienced. It was truly heart-breaking to witness the typhoon and the devastation it left behind.

Actually being there has a much greater impact than just seeing images on a TV screen.

I never want to experience anything like that again, and that is why I felt I needed to do something to help the poor victims of circumstance in the Philippines.

Shortly afterwards, I had a great vision about writing a book about football legends. The proceeds of the book's sales will go to help the victims.

The founder and P.R. manager of our talented team, Philippine United F.C., Leo Jensen, has also raised money for the typhoon victims.

The two very helpful ladies who helped me with my research at the Manila library: Susan A. Fetalcot, and Mayette A. Valdez.

Philippine United

Leo and I have known each other for going on five years now.

When Steve and I were coaching in Manila in 2009, the President of the Philippines Football Federation, Mari Martinez, asked me to contact Leo Jensen, who is Danish and now living and working in Manchester, England.

Mari Martinez wanted me and Leo to put together a men's team in England, with players who had Philippine and English dual nationality.

The reason behind Mari Martinez's thinking was quite simply to find Filipino players who would be eligible to play for the Philippines' national team.

Having a dual passport and a British mother or father would allow footballers to play for the Philippines. Almost every kid in England grows up with the desire to play football, (unlike in the Philippines, where basketball is their main sport).

Young players who have been brought up in England have football running through their veins, and so my colleague Mari thought that if they found players born in England, they would have the English passion for the game, and would be better equipped in every department, mentally and physically.

Mentally, because England invented the game of football many years ago and it is something that every kid grows up with, and physically, because the English are a much taller nation than the Filipinos so the players would be taller and stronger.

Mari's concept was very clever to say the least, and you only have to look now at the present Philippine national football team, the Azkals to see the results.

He always said to me that the foreign Filipino players always had a different mentality towards football. The Azkals now include quite a few foreign players, from England, and other European countries such as Germany and Holland. The overseas Filipino players are much taller and stronger than the locals.

It was a master stroke, and so with the help of my assistant coach, Steve Conroy, Leo and I formed Philippine United. Leo organized everything from getting the team into the West Hertfordshire League to all the paperwork and advertising, while I organized the trials at Watford, having sixty players to choose from, finishing with a final squad of twenty-three players.

It was really funny when Leo and I first met in Glossop, near Manchester. He carried a book with him, full of English/Filipino players who'd contacted Leo about the trials. The book contained a profile and a photograph of every player, and Leo had been incredibly thorough, writing down what position they played in, their weight, height, character etc. It was really amazing, so Steve and I nicknamed it "The Book".

Leo held it like it was the original copy of the Holy Bible. I kept hinting at Steve to see if I could try to see the players' names, but Leo was guarding it with his life. He was a bit wary of me at first.

In the past, when Leo was trying to put another team together, he'd had dealings with another coach, who'd turned out to be a complete idiot and caused Leo a lot of problems, but that's in the past. Leo and I became great friends and colleagues.

It was amazing how Leo got so many players to turn up at the first trial. We even had one guy who actually came all the way from California, USA. Can you believe that? I swear it is 100% true. Unfortunately, he wasn't very good. I did feel for him, after showing such desire to get in our team, but we all admired his endeavour throughout the trials.

We eventually got our full squad, and as head coach, I felt very satisfied with the chosen players.

In our first season, we finished as runners-up in our division. We got promoted to division one and boasted a 100% home record, including cup games.

In our second season, we finished third in the division. We also won the Asian Cup, beating China in the final with a score of 4-1.

Every week, the referees would comment on the way we played, thrashing much bigger teams, week after week.

One of our players, Jason Arroyo, won a football speed contest at Arsenal's ground The Emirates, and won himself a trial with the mighty Barcelona.

I also asked the national team's head coach, Des Bulpin, to allow Jason to train and play with the Azkals, in which he played a few friendly games and managed to score in one game.

Just to let you all know how good our team was, that same player, Jason Arroyo, could not always command a regular place with Philippine United in our second season. He was a very good player, but I had even better players in his position, so you can see what a good team we had.

I also got a call from a player who wanted to join Philippine United, and when he told me who he had played with in the past, I immediately rang the Philippines Football Federation (PFF) President Mari Martinez about him. I advised Mari to put the player straight into the Azkals side, which were due to play in the Maldives in a few weeks' time. Mari did play him. He was an instant hit, and that player is now Azkals' regular defender, Rob Gier.

The best part of being involved with Philippine United was not only that we'd put together a great team from scratch, but being directly involved in international football. The highlight of our short time together reached a climax when the PFF President Mari Martinez came over to England and actually stayed at Leo's house.

What Leo did, whilst Mari was in England, was a real stroke of genius because he called up half of the Premiership managers, asking them if we could meet them individually at one of their games, telling them that we were running a nursery team to the Philippines' national squad and that we were hosting the President of the Philippines Football Federation, who wanted to see what the Premiership was all about.

The four of us: Mari, Steve, Leo and I, met the managers and coaches of the Premier League clubs named below, and we were issued complementary match tickets to all the games and entry to every VIP lounge, including free food and drinks.

It was excellent what Leo achieved in such a short time – he's very resourceful when he puts his business head on. As my Granddad used to say: 'He can get where water can't.'

MANAGERS	CLUB
Sam Allardyce	Blackburn Rovers
Roberto Martinez	Wigan Athletic
David Moyes	Everton
Roy Hodgson	Fulham (present England manager)
Harry Redknapp	Tottenham Hotspur
Brian Marwood	Manchester City
Sammy Lee	Liverpool
Neil Warnock	Crystal Palace
Brian Laws	Sheffield Wednesday

We watched numerous games, ate good food, and met players and managers from the past and the present.

Leo was a great ambassador for Philippine United, and he really got the players revved up to meet Mari and for him to be at one or two of their games.

Mari was very impressed with the way our team performed, and said that he was really surprised at how skilful they were and how well they played together, even though they had only been together for a few months in total.

We really did have a very skilful team, with Raymond Tordecilla being our most talented player. I still think he would get a place in the Azkals team if he took the game seriously.

We also had a prolific striker in Anelio Mone. I was going to take him to Crystal Palace for a trial because my old mate Neil Warnock was manager there at the time. He would have done well there, but his attitude stunk.

I have never seen a more miserable footballer in my life. He scored forty-four goals in his first season with us but he was always giving someone a headache. He was only seventeen, and such a prospect, but with an attitude like that, there was no way I was putting my name on the line.

Me (centre), and Steve (front left), with Philippine United.

Our success was spreading through London in the local leagues, but we had one big major problem: funding.

Leo lived in Bolton in Greater Manchester, and Steve and I lived in Sheffield, but we played all our games in Watford, near London, which is a round trip of over three hundred miles every time. In two years of playing and training, we never missed a game and we never turned up late for any of the kick offs.

We needed to get a sponsor to help us with the petrol costs, and other things like balls and football strips.

Different people kept promising to help and sponsor us, but let us down in the end, so we had to give it up, after achieving so much in such a short time.

The team kept playing in the West Hertfordshire league, even though I was not coaching them anymore, but they never again achieved the same success, because when Leo had been the Club President, he'd been totally dedicated to developing the club.

Then Leo did it again, with a new Philippine United, a year later, in Manchester.

Leo organised trials for the new team. This time it was more local, with fewer expenses to pay.

Once again, I was head coach, with Steve as my assistant, but we had a slight problem regarding the league that Leo joined. The league officials said that we could not field an all-Filipino team, so we had to bring in other players to make the team up.

We had a decent line-up, but not quite as good as the Watford team. We had a real mixture of players.

They were mainly Filipinos, but we also had English, Dutch, and African players, including a brilliant goalkeeper from Libya, called Akrum Elsaadi. I wanted to place him with a professional club, but unfortunately, he had to return to Libya because he was only in the UK on a student visa.

He really was a special talent, and I knew that he was good enough for the Football League. If we'd had more time before he had to go home.

We were top of the league half way through the season, but then we lost some key players, such as our brilliant keeper. We started to lose a few games when the squad started arguing amongst themselves.

I was trying to pick my best eleven, but by doing that, I upset the Filipino regulars who were not as good as the new players that we'd brought in, which caused a conflict.

I tried to explain that we needed to win games, and use our substitutes accordingly, but the ring leaders of the so-called rebel group were having none of it. The disagreements reached a climax, and sadly, the team folded while it was at the top of the division.

One shining star from the Manchester team was a player called Mervin Evangelista, a fiery little winger with great ball control. He had great pace too. He could also score simple and spectacular goals. A player with so much potential – and he was still only seventeen years old.

One think I loved about young Mervin was that he always wanted to learn more about the game, and he would ask me a hundred questions in every training session.

I saw that he had talent and ambition, and so I took him under my wing and arranged for him to train with the national Philippine team's under-nineteens squad, the Young Azkals. Mervin gave a good account of himself too.

I arranged his trial and training with the Young Azkals through my good friend and colleague Leo Arnaiz, who took good care of him when he arrived in Manila. He told me that Mervin is a very good prospect for the future.

At the moment, Mervin is training with Stockport County. My friend Ian Lees, who runs the club's community foundation, tells me that Mervin is doing well there.

At this present time, I know that my dear friend Leo Jensen, also known as "Beauwolf" (for his Danish Viking background), is planning for us to start another new team of some sort, and knowing Leo as I do, I know he will succeed.

Now you all know why I have this bond with the Philippines and its people, and also why I want to help by doing something, like writing this book.

I'm really glad that I took this challenge upon myself. If you enjoy reading it, and I raise some money to help people whose lives have been destroyed by Typhoon Yolanda, it will have all been worthwhile.

CHAPTER TWO
RON ATKINSON

Ron, playing for Oxford United in the 1960s

I got hold of Ron by contacting his old club, West Bromwich Albion. They kindly sent me an email in return, with Ron's phone number.

To my delight, Ron was agreeable to meeting me for an interview. I called him to arrange the details. He lived down near Birmingham, but said that he would meet me in Peterborough.

He was going abroad to Tenerife the following day and his passport had run out.

Peterborough Passport Office is one of the places where you can get a new passport in person, like Liverpool.

Coincidentally, Ron was the manager of Peterborough United for a while. He still has strong ties with the club, especially with the main man there, Director Barry Fry, so Ron called him up and asked if he could use his office for the interview. Barry said yes, so that's where the interview took place.

We met Ron in the car park. They were looking for us, and we were looking for them. His driver was a stalwart Sheffield Wednesday fan, so I got on well with him straight away.

We met the secretary of Peterborough United, called Mary, who was very forthcoming and helpful, and she brought cups of tea for us all. She was a lovely woman. She told us to come down any time if we needed any help.

We went into the office and started the interview. It took a while to get comfortable and "set out our stall".

Ron was the first footballing legend I interviewed for this book. I thought it went very well, which was a good omen for the rest of the footballers I was to interview.

Some things didn't run totally smoothly, and Ron was waiting to collecting his passport, but he generously gave me the time he had: a good thirty to forty minutes, and we did go through a lot of stuff. He was a sheer joy to interview, with laughs every minute!

Ron is a larger than life character for sure. His football management career should by no means be overlooked. He wasn't always successful, but on many occasions, he was responsible for massive improvements to his clubs' performance, and his clubs appeared in seven cup finals, along with other accolades.

Ron had numerous stories to tell, and I must say that none of them were boring either.

While I was talking to Ron, I noticed that he was a really laid-back character, prepared to open up any chapter in his past, whether it was good or bad.

It was a pleasure to talk to him frankly about the highs and lows of his football career.

⚽

To start at the beginning, Ron Frederick Atkinson was born in Liverpool on 18 March, 1939, but grew up in Birmingham, playing football outside with his friends and joining amateur clubs.

He started his playing career at his beloved Aston Villa, at the age of 17, in 1956. He didn't make the first team, but he told me frankly that his biggest influence in football was the Villa coach at that time, Jimmy Hogan.

Ron really emphasized how influential Jimmy Hogan was to him. He said that Jimmy taught him so much about the game that it made a big difference throughout the rest of his career, not just the way he played football, but the managerial and coaching side of the game too.

In 1959, Ron moved onto Oxford United, where he made over 500 appearances and was known to everyone there as

"The Tank", because he seemed like an unstoppable force of nature.

At that time, Ron became the first footballer to captain a club from the Southern League, and rise through three divisions of the football league, into the Second Division.

Ron told me that playing for Oxford was a very good learning curve, which stood him in good stead for the higher levels of the football league.

His first managerial job was in 1971: Kettering Town. Ron said that he enjoyed every minute of this job, although later in his career, he would manage clubs which were a lot bigger in status.

Becoming a manager at the very young age of thirty-two was an eye-opener, but Ron seemed to adjust to the role without too many problems. In his three years there, he was quite successful, leading the team to the Southern League Championship in 1973.

This led to a better job for Ron, managing Cambridge United in 1974, who won the Fourth Division in 1977.

Bigger clubs were taking notice of Ron, and his next move was to First Division West Bromwich Albion, in 1978, and in that year, the team finished third place in the league.

Ron went onto have three good years at West Brom, reaching the UEFA Cup Quarter Finals, and beating Manchester United 5-3 at Old Trafford on 30th December 1978.

During this time, Ron was the first manager in the league to regularly play three black footballers: Cyrille Regis, Brendon Batson and one of his all-time favourite players, Laurie Cunningham, who sadly died very young in a car accident. Ron dubbed his three star players "the Three Degrees".

The legacy of these players is due to be commemorated at West Bromwich, with a larger than life size bronze statue of them celebrating a goal, sculpted by Graham Ibbeson.

Ron moved on again to his biggest club yet, Manchester United, in 1981. A lot of people thought that "Big Ron", as he was widely known, was the right man for the job at Old Trafford. With his infectious ambitions and charisma, he soon gained the admiration of the Manchester Faithful.

The early eighties was also the start of a period when football started to gain a glossier and more glamourous image: the early stage of footballers becoming notorious for flashy cars and houses, supermodel girlfriends and jet-set excess and success. "Big Ron" fitted this image perfectly, with his chunky gold jewellery, coiffured hair and designer sunglasses.

Ron spent five years at Old Trafford, with Manchester United winning the FA Cup twice. He paid a record transfer fee at the time, £1.5 million for Brian Robson, from his old club West Brom.

A Panini sticker, with Ron managing Manchester United in 1986.

During that era, the wages of Division One Footballers started to rise dramatically. By 1982, a top flight Division One footballer could earn an average of £750 per week, (£2,347 in 2014). This is still peanuts in comparison to the average Premiership wage in 2014 but it was still a relatively huge increase back then.

Sponsorship deals for individual clubs and the football league started to become big business in the early eighties. At first, the BBC refused to broadcast games featuring sponsored shirts, but they relented in 1983. In the 80s, Manchester United were sponsored by electronics company Sharp.

In Ron's last full season at United, 1985-1986, Ron's team got off to a flying start, winning all ten games, but the team's form sadly dropped after Christmas. Manchester United finished fourth in the First Division.

Fans were disappointed, and started turning on Ron, with some of them rooting for his resignation. Rumours were going around that he would be replaced with Aberdeen Manager Alex Ferguson, but Ron carried on, starting the 1986-1987 season with high hopes that things would get better.

Then things went disastrously wrong, with a series of defeats, leaving Manchester United languishing second from the bottom in the First Division. Atkinson was under pressure, and he was sacked as manager in November 1986.

⚽

Ron returned to manage West Bromwich in 1987, which were now fighting to remain in the Second Division. Ron ensured that they stayed up, and the team started to look like promising contenders again.

A move abroad to manage Spanish side Atlético Madrid, tempted Ron away for a season. This move didn't go too well, as he clashed with volatile club president Jesús Gil, and he was sacked after just three months as manager, replaced by his former deputy manager Colin Addison at West Bromwich Albion. Ron accused Addison of 'stabbing him in the back'.

⚽

Happier times were to come, when Ron made my day, as well as a lot of other "Owls" fans, and he took over my beloved Sheffield Wednesday, in 1989.

Ron gave us our first silverware for many years, by winning the league Cup 1-0, against his old club Manchester United, while Sheffield Wednesday were still in the old Second Division. Wednesday were soon back in the First Division, under Ron's management.

The "Wednesdayites" loved "Big Ron", and were very sad to see him go in 1991, to his very own beloved club Aston Villa, who came knocking for him.

Ron told me that the club just looked more appealing to him, because it was just down the road from where he lived. Every day, on his way driving to Sheffield, he would pass the Villa training ground.

'Norm, can you blame me for choosing Villa when it's on my doorstep?' he told me. 'Sometimes you just don't want to drive up that f*cking motorway, especially when I can fall out of bed onto the training pitch. Taking the job at Villa meant no more driving up and down the motorway.'

This was the 1992-1993 season: the start of the FA Premier League, and Aston Villa took second place. In 1994, Villa won the Football League Cup. Surely he was on the top of his game?

The Aston Villa Chairman, Don Ellis, told the media that Ron Atkinson was one of the best three managers in the top division, but just two days later, in November 1994, Ron was sacked.

The ageing Villa side had started to struggle against relegation at the start of the season, and Ron found himself no longer at the helm of his home club.

Big Ron bounced back, and managed Coventry City, taking over in February 1995, where he stayed for over two years, keeping the "Sky Blues" in the Premier League, and bringing in high profile players such as Gordon Strachan, who became the manager, when Atkinson became Director of Football.

In November 1997, Ron returned to a struggling Sheffield Wednesday, and helped the side to return to form and steer clear of relegation from the Premier League, but his good work there was only for one season, as Sheffield Wednesday didn't give him a permanent contract.

Finally, he managed his last club in the football league, Nottingham Forest. Sadly, this wasn't a triumphant end to his career. The season ended with Forest's relegation, at the hands of Ron's old club, Aston Villa, on 16 May 1999.

Within hours, Ron announced that he would be retiring from football management.

On a funnier note, I have to mention a story about Ron's time at Nottingham Forest.

As Ron was making his managerial debut for Forest, playing at home at the City Ground against Arsenal, Ron got into the opposing team's dug-out, just before the game started. He didn't realise his mistake for a few minutes, until everyone started laughing.

I must admit, it is rather funny, but I can't laugh too loud, because I did something similar when I was playing in America, so I think I'll change the subject quickly.

⚽

After his own footballing days as "The Tank", and being well known as "Big Ron", Atkinson's other nickname, "Mr Bo Jangles" is still remembered to this day because of the flashy gold watches and bracelets that he used to wear at the matches. I think "Big Ron" suits him just fine.

When I asked him about present-day football, Ron mentioned a few of the so-called "hard men" of yesteryear, e.g. Billy Bremner, Dave Mackay, Ron Harris, and Roy Keane, who used to take the game by the scruff of the neck and compete for ninety minutes. These days, he thinks the game sadly lacks that kind of conviction, and to be quite honest, I agree with him.

In Ron's exact words: 'they've sanitized the game nowadays.'

Ron wasn't sure what his fondest memory of football was, because he'd had so many highs in the game.

He knew for sure which one was his worst memory: when he was at my beloved Sheffield Wednesday and they got relegated on 43 points, which is still a record today. Usually a team is safe with 40 points. 'No team has ever got relegated with a score of 43 points,' Ron said, still astonished.

When I asked Ron about his favourite club, he quickly relied, 'all of them'. I liked this, but he wasn't just being diplomatic. He had different highs with every team. He explained how much he'd loved being the manager of his first club, Kettering Town, not just the "big boys" like Manchester United.

❦☢

Since leaving football, Ron has had numerous presenting jobs on television and radio, from football commentary, to appearing on the chat show 'Room 101', to releasing a Christmas single, in 2002.

Unfortunately, Ron has become notorious for his racist remark in April 2004, about Chelsea player, Marcel Desailly on live TV, calling him a 'lazy, thick n*gg*r'.

Ron believed that the microphone was switched off at the time, but his comments were inadvertently broadcast live to various countries in the Middle East. Ron immediately apologised and resigned from ITV and the Guardian.

Believe me when I say this, but Ron Atkinson is not even 1% a racist. If you flip back a few pages here, you will see that Ron was the first, and I emphasize the word "FIRST" manager to field three black players at once in the top division, and he continued to field black players throughout that season, and in every other season of his career.

Almost every team that Ron managed had its share of black players, because he valued them as a good nucleus for the team.

When I told Ron that I was a Sheffield Wednesday fan, he said:

'Really? My old player, Carlton Palmer comes to my house almost every week and has a coffee and a chat with me.' A perfect example of how Ron has not got any prejudice in his makeup.

Since I have interviewed Ron, I have also interviewed two ex-Sheffield Wednesday players from Ron's era, and Carlton Palmer was one of them.

David Hirst was the other ex-player. They both said what a load of bullsh*t it was to call him a racist.

"Hirsty" said: 'Everybody says something that might sound racist at some point. It all depends on how people interpret it.'

Ok! Ron made a big mistake with his racist comment. A lot of people make comments of that nature, but it doesn't always mean that they are racists.

Sometimes a person might just come out with a negative statement at a certain time about a certain subject, but it doesn't mean that they should be branded for life.

I'm not saying that what Ron said was right by any means. I'm just saying that because of one comment, he's now effectively been banned from football punditry.

Unfortunately, that means that all football fans lose out. Television needs entertaining experts like Ron Atkinson.

⚽

Ron became famous for his use of "Ronglish", his own unique style of commentary, with expressions such as "Early Doors", "lollipops" and "full gun", and colourful footballing metaphors like "someone in the England team will have to grab the ball by the horns". Surely we need Ron, to rescue us from bland football commentary?

Ron told me that he's still quite busy, and involved with numerous projects. He's an ambassador with William Hill and broadcasts on 'The Punt' podcast, along with his old colleague, ex-player, Robbie Savage. He has also things going on in the footballing world of the Middle East.

In August 2013, Big Ron starred in 'Celebrity Big Brother'. I asked him, 'How did you find the show?'

'Lucrative,' Ron replied.

Finally, I asked Ron to name his favourite player.

'George Best,' Ron replied. 'He was as good as Messi, because Messi plays every week on carpets, and "Besty" had to play on mud-heaps.' He has a valid point.

He said: 'I remember when "Besty" came back from suspension and played for Manchester United away at Northampton in the FA Cup. He scored six goals on a pitch that was six inches deep in mud.' I remember that game, and he is absolutely correct.

Ron has been out of football now as a manager for over ten years, and I have to say that the game is a lot less enjoyable with guys like "Big Ron" missing from the touchlines.

I have been involved with football for many years, on and off, and if there is anything that comes to mind that the game is lacking, it is characters like Brian Clough, Bill Shankly, Tommy Docherty, and of course, Ron Atkinson.

Big Ron and me in Peterborough.

CHAPTER THREE
MEL STERLAND

Mel Sterland in his 1980s prime at Sheffield Wednesday

Mel and I have been friends for some years already. He was a pretty easy person to interview. I just had to pick up my phone!

I was so happy when Mel agreed to be interviewed for my book. He thought it was a great idea, and he was really flattered that I wanted to include him.

Mel lives in Sheffield too, so he was also going to be easier to find than most of the other football legends.

As Mel is very friendly and reliable, he agreed right away to the interview, and offered to meet me anywhere. That's just the kind of guy he is. He'll do a favour for everybody.

Mel agreed to come down to my place, as he wanted to visit my brother Maurice, who's not well, and see how he was going on, as Mel has been ill himself.

He rolled up one Monday morning at my house, with a big knock on the door and his cheerful personality.

Mel's the kind of guy who has a permanent smile on his face. He was a pleasure to be with and he's a joy to interview. We finished up jamming together on my saxophones – but that's another story!

Out of all the people I interviewed, Mel was the only one who came to my house, and it was a great meeting, in every respect.

⚽

Melvyn Sterland was born in Sheffield, Yorkshire, on 1 October 1961.

It is a dream comes true for any young, aspiring footballer to sign professionally with the club that he grew up watching, and Mel was lucky enough to start his career with his beloved Sheffield Wednesday.

He joined the club in 1978, and made his debut soon afterwards, seventeen years old, against Blackpool at Hillsborough, coming on as a substitute.

A week later, he made his full debut, against Hull City, playing away. Mel told me that out of all the great games he has played, his debut in Hull is his favourite game of all time.

Mel soon became popular with the Sheffield Wednesday fans, due to his great attacking runs down the line, and also because of the spectacular goals he scored.

Soon to follow was his famous nickname: "Zico". In those days, Mel had long flowing curly hair and a ferocious shot, just like the Brazilian star, Arthur Antunes Coimbra, known as Zico.

The fans started shouting, 'Zico! Zico!', and the name stuck with him throughout his career.

Mel scored forty-nine goals in just 347 appearances – and let's not forget a very important fact here. Mel played full-back, not centre-forward.

I asked him about his favourite goal of all time.

'The scorcher I scored against Crystal Palace for the Owls,' he said.

Mel's goal tally was incredible for a defender. Only the ex-Nottingham Forest and England full-back, Stuart Pearce, has a better goal ratio.

Then again, one of the best ever attacking full-backs, to my knowledge, is ex-Leeds United and England player, Terry Cooper.

Terry Cooper was great at going down the line, and he had great dribbling skills too, but he never scored a lot of goals for Leeds.

However, he did score the winning goal at Wembley for Leeds when they beat Arsenal in the League Cup Final back in 1968, a rare occasion.

⚽

Mel told me that when he was picked to play for the full England team in 1988, it was an unbelievable feeling

He was so proud of achieving that accolade. He just couldn't express to me how wonderful it made him feel. He played in a friendly game against Saudi Arabia, playing in Saudi. The game finished 1-1. Mel told me that he really enjoyed the game, although he was a little upset at the time because he didn't manage to stop the Saudis' goal.

Mel also played for the England Under Twenty Ones team seven times, scoring three goals. He treasures a winners' medal from the 1984 UEFA Championship.

Mel Sterland's great quality is that he never forgets the friends who helped his career along the road to success.

One of the people Mel remembers fondly was Charlie Wade, the scout at Sheffield Wednesday, who spotted Mel playing as a youngster, and later, helped to get Mel signed with the club.

The match against Saudi Arabia was the only full international game that Mel played with England. He gave the shirt he wore on that day to Charlie Wade as a thank you, a wonderful gesture.

Mel had ten good years with the "Owls", but he told me that his best season at Hillsborough was when they had just got promotion into the old First Division with all the so-called, "Big boys".

Mel had a great season, playing almost every game, and he scored an incredible eight goals. The team finished fifth in the league, which qualified them to play in Europe in the UEFA Cup.

However, because all English teams were banned from any European competitions because of the Heysel Disaster in 1985, Sheffield Wednesday sadly never got the chance to play in the Cup.

While I was interviewing Mel in my lounge, he noticed a framed poster on my wall.

It was for the European Cup Tie match that I played in Germany in the 1977/78 season with Maltese team Sliema Wanderers, against the mighty Eintracht Frankfurt.

Mel asked me about it, and I said it was a great experience playing both legs, home and away, but I told him that I would have loved to have played at the top level in England, like he'd done.

Mel confided that he would have loved to play in Europe like me.

⚽

All through the interview we were having such a laugh, talking about old mutual friends. We've known each other for quite some time now, and every time we meet, all we do is laugh. Mel is always jolly and so pleasant to be around.

In 1989, the mighty Glasgow Rangers paid a fee of £800,000 for Mel, but his time there was not good, to say the least. He was only at the club for four months, playing in nine games, where he scored three goals.

He told me that he really loved the set-up at Rangers, and loved playing there, but he said that the manager, Graham Souness, just didn't like him, for some unknown reason.

Mel told me about the time he arrived at the club for training wearing a green tie. 'Norm, I dropped a right f*cking b*ll*ck. No one at Rangers ever wears anything green because of their biggest rivals, Celtic!'

Things just didn't pan out for Mel in Glasgow, so he came south again.

That same year, Mel signed for Leeds United, teaming up again with his old Sheffield Wednesday manager Howard Wilkinson.

Just as he did at Hillsborough, Mel became an instant favourite with the Elland Road fans.

Once again, Europe eluded him again, because even though Leeds qualified for Europe in 1990, finishing fourth, only the Winners and Runners-Up could play in European competitions, so once again, poor Mel missed out.

I asked Mel about one of his Leeds teammates on that Championship winning team, Eric Cantona.

Mel does not very often criticize people, but I can assure you that he did not like Eric Cantona. He said that he was very arrogant and a total bighead.

I got a total surprise when I asked Mel to name his favourite player of all time. Mel told me that his favourite player had always been Sheffield Wednesday's Tommy Craig.

When I asked him why him, Mel just said he was a player that he had always admired. I remember watching little Tommy Craig play for the Owls myself, and he was a bit special, I must say, but I always thought he was slightly timid, and he did not like getting kicked.

Mel told me a funny story about Tommy Craig. He met Tommy a few years ago and asked him for his autograph.

Tommy Craig recognised Mel right away.

'Are you taking the f*cking piss?' Tommy said.

I couldn't stop laughing. Obviously Tommy Craig wondered why a big star wanted an autograph from an old player like him.

Mel won the League Title for the old First Division (now The Premier League) in the 1991/92 season, and stayed at Leeds for another three seasons, having had five good years there.

An ankle injury forced Mel to retire in 1994, but he told me that he enjoyed every minute of his time at Leeds, just as he did at Sheffield Wednesday.

I asked Mel to name his hardest opponent

Mel replied that the dirtiest player, who injured him in good style, was ex-West Brom player Richard "Asa" Hartford. However, his most difficult opponent was Liverpool's John Barnes:

'He was so quick, and tricky with the ball.'

Mel's favourite football manager is Howard Wilkinson, who helped Mel through some bad times as well as the good ones at Leeds United.

Mel's favourite football club is obviously his very own Sheffield Wednesday.

⚽

After Mel retired, he managed a few Non-League clubs for a few years, and then had some bad luck with his health.

He woke up one morning with his ankle swollen, and it got worse, causing a blood clot.

Mel openly admitted to me that he was very scared at the time. He almost died.

He is now classed as disabled and can never work in football again, or do any other kind of work, so I do feel for him.

I told him about ex-players finding a lucrative career as after-dinner speakers.

'You'd be great at it, Mel.'

He just said: 'Norm, I can't do anything at all.'

I wish I could persuade him. I think he'd be perfect doing that, because he's so crazy and funny.

He told me that he can only fly for periods of two hours with his illness. He knows I coach regularly in the Philippines and he says that he'd love to go out there with us sometime, but unfortunately, his illness rules him out.

He can walk fine, but he gets out of breath quickly because one of his lungs is now damaged, and he finds it's very hard to breathe, especially when he's walking up hills.

⚽

Mel sometimes goes to Hillsborough to watch "the boys", but he thinks that footballers nowadays don't play with the same passion as they used to.

'It's a different game now, and I don't miss playing at all.'

He dislikes the way that football has almost transformed itself into a non-contact sport.

Mel Sterland is one of football's biggest characters, in every sense of the word. He is loved in Sheffield everywhere. I even know a few Sheffield United fans who love him

The game needs players like "Zico", and I do know for a fact that Sheffield Wednesday needs someone like him right now.

Mel was a real joy to interview, probably because we know each other pretty well so I didn't have to be careful about my questions.

Mel Sterland is simply a lovely warm human being and in writing about him in my book, the pleasure was all mine.

Mel and I get the saxophones out!

CHAPTER FOUR
EDDIE GRAY

EDDIE GRAY
LEEDS UNITED
INSIDE LEFT

A bubble-gum card featuring a young Eddie Gray in the 1960s.

I first met Eddie when he was an apprentice professional at Leeds United, signed by Don Revie.

My brother Maurice and I had just signed for Leeds United as fourteen-year-old schoolboys.

Getting signed by one of England's top clubs was a really big deal, and we were invited to Elland Road.

We were brimming with excitement, that sunny spring bank holiday day, as our parents drove us to Leeds. We arrived at the training pitch and we'd just come into the dressing room, when Eddie and two other Leeds youngsters, Jimmy Lumsden (now a top football coach) and Ian Lawson, walked in.

Eddie shook my hand. I was thrilled. The memory is vivid, even though it's almost fifty years ago.

On our first meeting with Leeds United, we ended up as golf caddies, as a round or two of golf was a normal activity for the players, once they'd trained in the morning.

The fact that I had known Eddie during my time at Leeds United made him an ideal interviewee for this book.

Eddie was more than happy to oblige when I called him up. I was certain that he would have many interesting stories and opinions, as he remained in the game after retiring, managing Leeds, Whitby and Hull City, and becoming a football pundit on TV and radio.

I reminded Eddie about our first meeting, which he remembered fondly. I asked him about Ian Lawson, as I always thought that he was a special talent. Unfortunately, a knee injury meant an early end to his career at Leeds United. He lives in Ireland now.

Before we interviewed Eddie for this book, we met him at Elland Road again. He was doing a news item for Yorkshire Television, as he still works for Leeds United.

It was good to watch Eddie in action, and after ten minutes, we all moved onto the nearby Commercial Inn, run by another ex-Leeds player, Peter Lorimer.

The interview took a while to get going, because Eddie and Peter were catching up with each other, but we had a great time. Eddie is a great lad, forthcoming and helpful.

Edwin "Eddie" Gray was born in Glasgow, Scotland on the 17th of January 1948.

Eddie played for Scotland Schoolboys, and hoped that he would sign for his local favourites, Celtic.

However, it was not meant to be, and instead, Eddie came south of the border and signed professionally for Leeds United in 1965. He stayed with the club for his whole playing career, which spanned three decades.

Don Revie was the new manager at Leeds when he signed Eddie, taking over at the club when they were almost at the foot of Division Two.

Leeds United weren't there for long. Revie put a team together that would be remembered for many years to come. The very next year, Leeds United won promotion to the top flight in Division One, with all the "Big boys".

One of Revie's changes was to ditch Leeds' traditional blue and yellow kit and adopt an all-white strip, just like Real Madrid, but it was his skill at picking gifted players that made the team a success.

Eddie didn't waste any time getting into the first team. With his silky dribbling skills, Don Revie realised that the teenage Eddie was a very special talent.

Once Eddie made his debut, everyone knew that he was a real star in the making.

⚽

Eddie Gray spent his entire playing career at Leeds United, spanning almost twenty years, which these days would very rarely happen.

He played his last game for Leeds in 1983.

In total, he appeared in almost 454 games and scored fifty-two goals.

Eddie had a wonderful career at Leeds, helping to win numerous trophies for his team:

Football League Division One Winners: 1968/69.

Runners-up: 1966, 1970, 1971, and 1972.

FA Cup Winners: 1972.

Runners-up: 1970 and 1973.

FA Charity Shield Winners: 1969.

Runners-up: 1974.

Football League Cup Winners: 1968.

Inter-Cities Fairs Cup Winners: 1968 and 1971.

Runners-up: 1967.

European Cup, runners-up: 1975.

After Eddie finished playing, he had various managerial jobs, starting at Leeds United from 1982-85.

He then moved on to little Whitby Town, from 1985-86. Shortly afterwards, he moved to Rochdale, from 1986-88, and then over to Hull City from 1988-89.

Finally, he moved back to Leeds United as caretaker manager for a year, in 2003-2004.

❀❂

Eddie in action in his all-white Leeds kit.

As you can see, Eddie Gray had quite an illustrious career, winning lots of trophies and being remembered for two of the greatest goals ever seen on television.

I'm referring to the goals he scored against Burnley in 1970. It was a regular league match, but there was nothing regular about the two goals he scored.

Eddie got the ball on the half-way line, and seeing Burnley's keeper several yards off his line, he decided to lob the ball over fifty yards. It landed over the keeper and dropped into the back of the net. This was no fluke!

Having amazed the crowd with this skilful display, the second goal was even more spectacular. This goal has gone down in football history as one of the greatest ever! The ball came to Eddie at the edge of the box. In spite of being crowded by the Burnley defence, Eddie found room to manoeuvre his way round each of them, turning on an area the size of a sixpence, ultimately passing five defenders and coolly placing the ball on the back of the net. Surely this was one of Eddie's favourite moments?

Believe it or not, but when I asked Eddie to name the favourite goal of his career, he didn't state the obvious choice, his amazing goals against Burnley. Eddie named the goal he had scored on his debut, against my much-loved Sheffield Wednesday.

That was his all-time favourite game too, his first ever game as a professional footballer, aged just seventeen.

Another of Eddie's favourite games was the Centennial Cup-Final against Arsenal, in 1972.

I can't forget that day either. I had a ticket to watch the game with my brother Maurice, but I couldn't make it. I had just signed a three year contract with the Greek Australian team Pan Hellenic FC, and at the moment the match kicked off, I was on a plane to the other side of the world.

The other game that sticks in Eddie's memory is the away game in the Semi-Final of The European Cup, against Barcelona in 1975.

'They had such great players – especially the formidable Johan Cruyff!' Eddie told me.

Obviously, he also loved the two games he played with Leeds United against Celtic, especially the game played away at Celtic Park. The stadium was literally packed to the rafters, with 138,000 fans inside.

Eddie also told me that winning the Division One title in 1968/69 was his greatest achievement.

Football fans always seem to remember Eddie's performance in the 1970 Cup-Final against Chelsea, in which he tormented fullback David Webb for the whole 90 minutes.

I also asked him who his hardest opponents were.

'There were quite a few!' he laughed.

He named Ron Harris, Eddie McCredie, Tommy Smith, and the aptly named Peter "Assassin" Storey.

'They all liked to "dish it out", kicking anything that moved!'

Unfortunately, because of all the so-called "Hard men" at that time, and more lenient referees, Eddie sustained lots of injuries, which is the main reason why he only played twelve times for Scotland. I couldn't believe it when he told me that.

Don Revie wouldn't let Eddie play mid-week games for Scotland because of the risk of him getting injured. He then wouldn't be available for Saturday's game for Leeds.

I suppose you couldn't blame Mr Revie for doing that, especially as Eddie was pretty injury-prone

Skilful players will always get kicked, and let's face it, Eddie Gray was certainly one of the most skilful players around at that time for sure.

Eddie said that his absence from his national team was no big loss, because at that time, Scotland had an abundance of wingers like Charlie Cooke, Willie Johnson, Willie Morgan,

Willie Henderson, John Robertson, and one player whom Eddie had a lot of praise for, Tommy Hutchinson.

⚽

What happened to all those great Scottish players? Why doesn't Scotland produce talent like that anymore?

Eddie told me that when Celtic won the European Cup in 1966, not only were all the Celtic players Scottish, but they were also all from Glasgow – within a fifteen miles radius of the stadium, which is quite incredible.

'It was a really great era for football,' Eddie said. 'There were lots of brilliant players in every team.'

There are still great players around in The Premiership, but like most other players of "yesteryear", Eddie feels that we have too many overseas players in top teams, and it's obviously affecting our home-grown talent.

Eddie recalled a recent visit back to Glasgow. In his youth, kids would play fifteen-a-side, on any spare ground, but on his recent visit to Glasgow, he said that he didn't even see one kid playing with a ball.

Eddie is also not too keen on the academies these days, because they don't allow kids to play for their school.

I agree 100% with Eddie.

School football is where it all begins, and it is a necessary part of the development of young players.

It's a phenomenon that many of the great players of the world today come from impoverished areas of Africa and South America.

Eddie and I agree that too many youngsters in the Western World are hooked on computer games, and don't spend their spare time kicking a ball around like we did.

Eddie is not an idealist. He just speaks from the hip and quite frankly, he does talk a lot of sense.

In the year 2000, Eddie was voted "The third best ever player for Leeds United of all time." He certainly has a legacy of some memorable football moments.

One thing Eddie might not be remembered for is that in his twenty year playing career, he was never booked once. I for one, think that is quite amazing, considering the kicks he used to get. He's a true gent.

⚽

Eddie is still at Leeds United, working on the LUTV and doing football commentary work on Yorkshire Radio as well. Eddie is an ambassador for the club too, and he told me that he never misses a game for Leeds, home or away.

However, he admits that the team now is a far cry from the great Leeds team of old.

Eddie Gray is a true legend.

Not only at Leeds United, where fans even today still love and admire him, but everywhere in the football world.

People will always remember EDDIE GRAY.

All smiles, with Eddie Gray

CHAPTER FIVE
KEN WAGSTAFF

Ken Wagstaff:
Action-packed at Hull City.

I was lucky enough to meet Ken through Geoff Barmby, who used to play with him at Hull City.

I'd written to Hull City, and they passed my letter onto Geoff, who got in touch with me.

Incidentally, Geoff Barmby's son, Hull Player Nick Barmby, was an England international not so long ago. Geoff kindly gave me Ken Wagstaff's number, which was a good stroke of luck!

When I called Ken, he sounded a little apprehensive at first, but it turned out to be one of my best interviews. We laughed solidly for two hours.

Instead of meeting in Hull, Ken suggested that we should meet in a tiny little town called Hessle, near Hull. I'd never been there before.

We met one Tuesday lunchtime, in a beautiful medieval-looking town square, and held our interview in a lovely old pub, called the Marquis of Granby. It has a great restaurant, with football pictures on the wall, featuring Nick Barmby in his Hull City kit.

The pub had probably had a photo of Ken too, but it must have been taken down because it was too old! (I'm only joking, Ken!)

Ken was accompanied by his friend Mick, a very nice guy who is a trawler fisherman. He had some interesting tales of his own as well!

⚽

Ken Wagstaff was born in Langwith, Nottinghamshire, on 24 November, 1942.

He joined his local team, Mansfield Town in 1960, at the age of 17, and he quickly started to score on a regular basis in the youth side.

Mansfield's manager at the time, Raich Carter, noticed his quick progress, and slotted Ken into the first team.

Ken scored twice on his debut, and went on to score a very credible ninety-three goals in 181 appearances, which is a great scoring ratio of a goal every two games.

In 2007, he was voted by Mansfield Town fans as their "All-time favourite player".

Meanwhile, other clubs were taking notice of Ken's performances. In 1964, Hull City paid £40,000 for Ken, a club record at that time. Ken moved on, to new and better pastures.

The Hull City fans loved him right from the start, and Ken rose to the challenge, scoring a grand total of 173 goals in 378 appearances, keeping up his scoring rate of one goal in almost every two games, at a much higher level of football.

In Hull's promotion year, 1966, Ken scored 31 goals in total for that season, his best record so far.

As part of Hull City's centenary celebrations in 2005, supporters voted Wagstaff "the best Hull City player of all time", and in 2007, fans voted him their "all-time favourite player".

To this day, no other footballer has won this award twice, with two different clubs. It's a fine achievement by any standards.

I think it goes to show how popular Ken was with fans at both clubs where he played.

Ken hung his boots up in 1976, after sustaining a serious knee injury while playing for an Australian team, Sunshine George Cross Football Club, in Melbourne.

He told me that he misses playing very much. He loved getting paid for something that he loved doing.

Ken was a little conservative at first in our interview, but as we moved on with different topics, he warmed up and his sense of humour shone through. I could see why he was such a well-liked person at the clubs he played for.

I can see, by my own experience of talking to Ken, that he was one of the game's real characters, and I just knew that I had to have him in my book. He did not disappoint me. He had me laughing from beginning to end, telling story after story.

⚽

I asked Ken if he had any regrets about not playing in the top flight division.

'Not at all,' he said. 'I played against First Division teams in various cup games, but I wasn't too impressed with them, and I honestly found that the opposing defenders didn't trouble me any more than the defenders I was playing against week after week in the lower division.'

He also told me that the infamous Brian Clough had wanted to sign him on a couple of occasions, but the Hull Chairman would not sell him. That's why "Cloughie" bought Kevin Hector, because Hull City would not let Ken leave.

Ken said that he was quite happy to stay at Hull anyway, especially because he loved playing alongside his striking partner and good friend Chris Chiltern.

The pair of them took their opponents' defences apart, week after week. Ken could not praise Chris Chiltern enough, and said that he was a complete joy to play with.

Without hesitation, Ken confirmed that his favourite player of all time was Chris Chiltern. I think to give that accolade to your team mate is rather special.

Once, Chris Chiltern was asked by a reporter if he'd had any bad injuries while playing with Hull City. Chris replied that he'd had approximately 260 stitches, a smashed jaw, numerous leg injuries, a smashed face, a damaged back, and many other injuries he couldn't remember.

The same reporter then asked Ken the same question, and Ken answered: 'None at all hardly, mate. I didn't sign a contract stating that I had to get injured. I just let "Chilts" take the entire hammer for both of us.'

I couldn't stop laughing. Ken has a funny way of telling a good story, a bit like Ron Atkinson does.

Ken also said that "Chilts" was the finest header of a ball he had ever played with, as well as being very good with his feet too.

The finest ball-header that springs to my own mind was ex-Tottenham Hotspur striker Alan Gilzean. He was brilliant at any kind of headers, but that's just my opinion. Ron Davies of Southampton was also a great ball-header.

In Ken's opinion, Hull City's pitch, Boothferry Park, was the finest playing surface in the land. He loved playing there and scored many goals on it too.

Ken had a close relationship with his Hull team-mates. He liked playing with Ken Houghton, and especially Ian Butler, Hull's left winger.

'If we needed to waste time at the end of a game, we'd just give the ball to Butler – hardly anyone could get the ball off him!'

I asked Ken which defender gave him the hardest time when he was playing. Without hesitation, he said: 'Well, there weren't any defenders who really bothered me, but that b*st*rd who played for Norwich City, Duncan Forbes was always at my f*cking feet. He was a dirty b*stard. He kicked anything that moved. He would kick me from start to finish and in those days the refs let things go."

Ken Wagstaff and me in Hessle.

CHAPTER SIX
HARRY GREGG MBE

Harry Gregg in classic goal-saving mode.

I sent Harry a letter via Manchester United, and they kindly forwarded it on to him.

I was having my Sunday evening tea, and the phone rang. I said:

'Hello, who's this?'

I heard a voice with a pronounced Northern Irish accent say:

'Is that Norman?'

'Yeah, that's me, who's this?'

'Harry. Harry Gregg!'

As soon as I heard his accent, I knew it was him.

I was so elated to be talking to this very brave man, who'd saved a lot of lives in the Munich disaster.

We talked on the phone, and Harry said he would love to be interviewed. He was impressed that I was putting the book together for a good cause.

Harry was very keen, and very forthcoming. It would have been great to visit him. Unfortunately for me, he lives in Coleraine in Northern Ireland. It's right at the top of the country, in County Londonderry. He said that I was very welcome to come for a visit, but it's a very long way to go for a short interview.

We arranged to have a longer "chinwag" on the phone instead. We'd already been talking for half an hour!

Harry is a real character, with lots of funny stories.

On the serious side, he didn't mind talking about the Munich Air Disaster either.

I arranged to call him again in a couple of days. That time, we spoke for about two and a half hours, and had a really good conversation.

⚽

Harry Gregg was born in South Derry, Northern Ireland on 27 October, 1932.

Before he became a professional footballer, he worked as a carpenter, and Harry told me that was how he got his powerful physique.

In fact, we both chuckled about him being built "like a brick shithouse".

Harry didn't stay long on the tools, and in 1952, he was signed by Doncaster Rovers at the age of nineteen, and soon became known and loved as a great goalkeeper.

I didn't know that Harry had started his career at Doncaster, and he told me that playing for them was a good education. He played there under manager Peter Doherty.

Every now and then in our interview, Harry mentioned how the Doncaster boss had taught him an incredible amount about the game, and how he was very instrumental in Harry's career. Harry played there until 1957, spending five great years with them, playing ninety-four games in all.

It was only a matter of time before the "Big guns" would come knocking on the door for his signature, as he was now a very accomplished keeper.

Manchester United paid £23,000 for Harry's services, and at that time it was a world record fee for a goalkeeper.

Little did I know, but my very own team, Sheffield Wednesday, had also made an offer of £18,000 for Harry. However, fate decreed that he went to United.

Harry had only been at the club for three months when he was caught up in one of the most horrendous tragedies in the history of football.

❦

It was February the 6th 1958.

The previous day, Manchester United had played the second leg of the Quarter-Final tie in the European Cup, away to Red Star Belgrade. United had drawn 3-3, putting them through to the semi-final, to play Milan.

Returning from Yugoslavia, the plane needed to stop for refuelling in Munich. As the plane attempted to take off for Manchester, the treacherous weather conditions worsened.

The Airspeed Ambassador aeroplane had already failed twice at take-off.

Despite the snow, the pilot, Captain James Thain, was keen to avoid an overnight stay in Munich.

On the third attempt, the plane skidded on the slush covering the runway and crashed into the fence surrounding the airport and across the road, before colliding with a house, a tree and a hut containing tyres and fuel, which exploded on impact.

The crash claimed twenty three lives. Eight of them were Manchester United players.

TOMMY TAYLOR

MARK JONES

EDDIE COLEMAN

DAVID PEGG

ROGER BYRNE

GEOFF BENT

LIAM WHELAN

DUNCAN EDWARDS (who died 16 days later)

Harry explained that he had the greatest respect for Captain James Thaine.

He was blamed solely for the crash, with allegations that he had not cleared ice from the wings of the plane.

However, after a full inquiry into the disaster, in 1968, Thaine was eventually cleared of all responsibility for the crash.

The build-up of slush on the runway was confirmed to be the cause of the accident.

I was quite surprised at Harry when I mentioned the Munich Disaster.

He didn't mind talking about it at all. He has probably been asked about that dreadful night so many times, that he's become thick-skinned about it.

He really played down his heroic actions that day. He said: 'I just acted instinctively, and ran into the wreckage, wanting to save as many people as I could.'

Harry rescued numerous team mates, including Bobby Charlton, Jackie Blanchflower, Dennis Violet, and a pregnant woman, Vera Lukić, the wife of the Yugoslav diplomat, and her baby daughter

When Harry found out that his home town was planning to erect a statue in his honour, he just couldn't believe it. Harry wasn't very comfortable about it.

He said: 'Norman, I never wanted a statue or any praise of any kind for what I did. I just did what any person would have done in the same circumstances.'

I personally don't agree with Harry. I don't think that most people would have run into that burning plane without hesitation, bringing people to safety. He really meant what he said. I could sense the sincerity in his voice.

I was also in Munich, a short time ago. I only thought about the crash when I was leaving Munich for Manchester.

We were still on the runway, getting ready to take off when it hit me. As I thought about the 1958 Munich Disaster, I swear a cold shiver went through me like a knife.

My friend Shaun Rycroft, who was with me at the time, looked at me and asked me if I had seen a ghost.

I told him the whole story and he couldn't believe it. Nowadays, Munich airport has moved, but I will never forget the feeling I had when I realised the circumstances.

⚽☺

Harry, and Bobby Charlton, are the only two Manchester United Aircrash survivors who are still alive.

I guess when something like that happens to you, it will stick with you for life.

Harry was awarded the MBE for his bravery in Munich, and he told me he was even shy about accepting his award from royalty, because he really did think that what he did was a normal thing that others would have done.

He did like being at Buckingham Palace though. He thought it was rather grand, and he even saw Eric Clapton there too receiving an award, but I will not tell you what he said about him. I wish I could share the story with you but I fear that Harry would kill me!

Harry told me a few stories about the aftermath of the crash, but he told me they were just between him and me, and obviously I would not break his trust. However, I must admit that I was shocked at what he told me.

⚽

Back in Manchester, it was decided that "the show must go on". Manchester United were due to play their fifth round Cup-Tie, against none other than my very own Sheffield Wednesday.

Manchester United won the tie 3-0, with a hurriedly assembled squad of players made up of youth and reserve team members.

The makeshift Manchester United team even reached the Cup Final against Bolton Wanderers, but they lost 2-0, with Nat Lofthouse fouling Harry Gregg to score his second goal of the game.

✦☉

A couple of years later, United were playing away against Luton Town. After the match had finished, a Luton fan ran on the field. Harry punched him in the face and knocked him out cold.

The fan was taken to hospital for his injury, but Harry did not get charged with bad conduct. It was said that he had been provoked all through the game, so Harry got off "Scott free".

Harry told me that he had some wonderful times at Old Trafford, but in the nine years that he played there, the nearest he got to winning a trophy was the Runners-up medal from the match against Bolton in that 1958 FA Cup-Final.

Harry played a total of 247 games for United, and left in 1966 to play for Stoke City.

As Harry was about to leave United, another Northern-Irishman was just starting his career there. He used to clean Harry's boots. He was none other than George Best.

Harry signed for Stoke City after leaving United, for an undisclosed fee.

I asked him Harry about his favourite game. He said it was the Home International game, between England and Northern Ireland at Wembley, with Ireland winning 3-2. It was special to Harry for two reasons: it was the first time an Irish team had beaten England at Wembley, and secondly, because three players in that England squad were his Manchester United team mates who later died in Munich: Roger Byrne, Tommy Taylor, and the brilliant young Duncan Edwards.

Harry told me that he'd really loved those Home Internationals, and really missed them. I remember them fondly too.

Harry played 25 times for Northern Ireland. In 1958 at the World-Cup Finals in Chile, Harry was voted "The Best Goalkeeper of the Tournament".

⚽

When I asked Harry about his favourite "save" of all time, he just said:

'None really. I always thought that every save was as important as the next.'

I got an immediate answer without any hesitation, when I asked him about his favourite all-time player:

'Without a doubt, Peter Doherty – the ex-Northern Ireland International. He had everything that a footballer needed.'

Harry kept praising Peter, and said that he was a wonderful manager at Doncaster, teaching Harry lots about the game, and helping him to turn into a great goalkeeper.

The best player Harry had seen at Manchester United was George Best. Harry respected late, great Sir Stanley Matthews too:

'What a brilliant player he was to watch!'

⚽

Harry only stayed at Stoke for a year. A short time afterwards, in 1968, he took his first managerial job, at Shrewsbury Town.

That's where I met Harry for the first and only time. My brother Maurice was playing for Harry at the time, and I was invited to train with them for a few days.

I must say, I was treated with great warmth and acceptance from the Shrewsbury players and management.

Harry really loved being at Shrewsbury, and what a coincidence it turned out to be for him.

Chairman Yates of Shrewsbury Town had been in the RAF in World War Two. He had been the navigator for Captain Thaine, the pilot of the ill-fated Munich disaster aeroplane.

The two men developed a great friendship and understanding for a few years, until 1972, when Harry felt that the board was taking too many decisions about the buying and selling of players. The tension drew to a head, and Harry could not stand it anymore, so he parted ways with the club.

The dispute was mainly because of a certain swap-deal with West Bromwich Albion.

The Shrewsbury player involved was centre-half Alf Wood. Harry had always played him in defence but even though Alf played at the back, he scored eighteen goals in one season, so Harry played him up-front as a centre-forward. He finished the season with a total of forty-two goals, which any striker would be proud of.

West Brom wanted to swap an unknown kid, a centre-back, for Alf Wood, and Harry did not like the situation one little bit.

Little did Harry know at the time, but the so-called "unknown" turned out to be a full Scottish International, who later, joined Manchester United. That player was Jim Holton.

The funny part of this story is in a poem about the player, which Harry recited to me, laughing at the same time:
"SIX FOOT TWO
EYES OF BLUE
BIG JIM HOLTON'S
AFTER YOU."
After Harry had finished he said with a loud chuckle in his voice:
'Eyes of blue – you must be f*cking joking. His eyes were as brown as the sh*t in the street.'

I laughed too, when he told me that.

⚽

What I love about Harry is that he has a wonderful energy about him. Even at 82 years old, he's so active with his answers and explains things vividly.

Harry told me lots of tales about numerous football clubs and players. Unfortunately, I'm not at liberty to speak about them, but I can tell you now that a few of them would open your eyes.

Harry's hardest opponent was Tottenham Hotspur's Bobby Smith. Harry said he was the toughest centre-forward that he had ever seen or played against.

If anyone wanted to mix it with Smith, they would usually come off worse, as Harry did on numerous occasions.

'He was a great player – totally underrated,' recalled Harry.

Harry always took notice of his opponents, and rated Bobby up there with the greats.

Coming a close second in terms of toughness was Bolton's Nat Lofthouse, who Harry also rated highly, apart from that time in the 1958 final when Harry was fouled when Lofthouse scored Bolton's second goal.

⚽

The second club that Harry managed was Swansea City, from 1972-75. Then he moved on to manage Crewe Alexandra from 1975-78. After having a break for a few years, Harry finished his managerial career with Carlisle United, from 1986-87.

Harry did go back to Manchester United as their goalkeeping coach, but after three years, the United manager, Ron Atkinson, told Harry that he wouldn't be needing his services anymore.

⚽

As you can see, Harry Gregg MBE had a wonderful and colourful career in football, playing and managing too.

He is genuine legend, and a great person to interview. He kept me laughing for over two hours, and it didn't seem to matter that we were doing the whole interview by phone.

Harry really is a total gentleman.

I know that he swears like a trooper, but only to make a situation sound funnier, just as I do myself.

I must say that it was a great pleasure to talk to "The Hero of Munich".

I know he will curse me for calling him that, but it happens to be true. He was, and will remain a hero, for many, many years to come.

Harry Gregg – a true football legend.

CHAPTER SEVEN
CARLTON PALMER

Carlton Palmer still lives in Sheffield, and by coincidence, we actually go to the same gym.

I'd talked to Carlton about the book, and he thought it was a really good idea. He supports lots of charities too. Carlton told me his email address, but I didn't write it down, as we were in the gym at the time, and I didn't have a pen! I tried to email him, but it bounced back, so I hoped I'd bump into him again in the gym.

Carlton Palmer playing for England in the 1990s.

A few days later, I was interviewing his fellow Sheffield Wednesday team-mate, David Hirst, at the Sheffield Beauchief Hotel.

I was due to meet David in the wine bar underneath the hotel, which is nice and quiet at midday.

When I walked in there, guess who David was having a drink with? Carlton Palmer!

I did a "double-whammy" interview, and it turned out great.

It was a really good interview, with each of them bouncing off each other.

⚽

Carlton Lloyd Palmer was born in Rowley Regis, on 5 December 1965.

He started playing for his much loved West Bromwich Albion 1984, after leaving school. Carlton had always loved West Brom from a very early age and had watched them whenever he could.

When the chance came to play for his childhood idols, he grabbed it with both hands. He had five good years at the "Hawthorns", learning his trade, and he scored four goals in 121 appearances.

⚽

Carlton moved up north to Sheffield Wednesday in 1989, for a fee of £750,000.

He quickly adapted and was a regular feature in the Wednesday midfield, week after week. In 1992, he got his first England call-up.

Carlton played for England eighteen times, scoring one goal.

He scored fourteen goals for the Owls in 205 appearances. Carlton told me that he really loved playing for the Owls and that they were the all-time favourite club that he'd ever played for.

Ron Atkinson was by far his favourite manager. When I interviewed Ron Atkinson, he said that he and Carlton are close friends, with Carlton calling round to his place almost every week. Ron said that Carlton had kept himself very fit: 'He could still play now,' Ron commented.

In 1993, Carlton played against Arsenal in the FA Cup Final, and the League Cup Final, with Arsenal winning both games.

After five great years at Hillsborough, Carlton moved to Yorkshire neighbours Leeds United in 1994, for a fee of just over £2,500.000.

He stayed at Leeds for three years, scoring five goals in 103 appearances.

⚽

Carlton moved on again, this time moving all the way down to Southampton for a fee of £1,000 000.

He stayed there for two seasons, scoring three goals in forty-five appearances.

Once again, he packed his boots and signed for Nottingham Forest for just over £1,000,000. Disapointingly, he managed to score just one goal in sixteen appearances.

The very same year, he moved again, to Coventry City, scoring again just the one goal and appearing in thirty games.

He also had loan spells at Watford in 2001 and his old club Sheffield Wednesday too, just afterwards.

⚽

In 2001, Carlton became Player/Manager for Stockport County. One thing I really admired about Carlton was that he was honest enough to admit that his time at Stockport was not a happy one.

On the other hand, because things were not going too well on the field, it meant that he wasn't scared to try new approaches.

He told me that he'd received a phone call from ex-Manchester United and England player Brian Robson, offering to help Carlton by giving a few training sessions and advice.

Some of Carlton's friends at the club thought that he was crazy to let Robson come down. They thought that if the team did well under Robson's guidance, Carlton might be out of a job. Carlton just replied:

'I'm not bothered about losing my job. If it helps my team in any way, then surely I can only benefit – and the team too.'

I liked Carlton's attitude towards accepting Robson's help. If he feared he was going to get the sack anyway, he thought "what have I got to lose?", and put the team first.

Carlton Palmer did get the sack at Stockport after two years at the club, and after a short break from the game, he became Manager of Mansfield Town in 2004.

He didn't stay long, due to getting too much abuse from the Mansfield fans, so he resigned in 2005. Mansfield Town was the last club Carlton was associated with.

⚽

After playing and managing football, Carlton has worked as a TV football pundit and sports reporter

Just like me, Carlton has also being doing some coaching in Asia.

Carlton had also got some new things in the pipeline that he is looking forward to doing in the near future.

He told me he has recently taken some time off, and he's enjoying it.

We did talk for a while about coaching and how it's changed, and how hard it is these days to get your coaching badges.

Carlton replied that he didn't know whether he could adapt to coaching after being a manager, but he does enjoy it. He also told me that he videos every coaching session, so that he can look back on it and show the players where they went wrong, because the video does not lie.

I agreed with him totally. I don't video my coaching sessions now, and haven't done so in the past, but it's a good idea. I can see the benefit of it if you have time, or have someone free to use the video camera in a coaching session.

We agreed that a lot of coaches who have all the top qualifications are sometimes useless on the field, and that some of the best coaches that we had both worked with had very few or no coaching qualifications at all, but did very well

I asked Carlton if he had any regrets and he said:

'Absolutely none. I've done everything that I wanted to do, and I'm still doing new stuff even now, so no – I don't regret anything at all.'

I ask Carlton to name his favourite player of all time.

'Without a shadow of a doubt, Paul Gascoigne,' he said.

Carlton couldn't name his favourite football match, because he'd had so many highs in his playing career.

We discussed racism in football. Carlton thinks the same way that I do about it: that things have gone too far, and that nowadays, you can't even blink the wrong way at someone. At times, it's totally ridiculous, with people making a fuss about nothing. A positive attitude is essential.

'I've been called everything over the years,' Carlton said. 'But it's no use moaning about it. You've just got to get on with it and laugh at them. That's the best way to stop racism.'

I asked Carlton to name his hardest opponent on the pitch.

'The original Ronaldo – when he was playing for the Dutch team PSV. He was amazing to play against.'

We discussed the differences in players today, compared with twenty years ago at the height of Carlton's career.

Carlton summed up the topic:

'I went down to Villa Park when Martin O'Neil was Villa's manager. I asked him where all the players were, and O'Neil said: 'Oh, just go down to the field – you'll see them there.' So I did, and the only players still playing and practicing were goalkeeper Brad Friedel, and Ashley Young, who now plays for Manchester United.'

Carlton said that footballers today don't seem to want to bond as a team, or work on extra training drills:

'They just want to leave as early as possible.'

Carlton told me that when he trained with West Brom when he was young, he had to catch two buses just to get to the ground, but he was glad to do it. Nowadays, young footballers get dropped off wherever they want. There's no togetherness whatsoever.

Carlton also commented that a lot of ex-professional footballers suffer from severe depression:

'Do you know, Norm, why they are all so f*cking depressed? It's because they don't have the f*cking money anymore. The lifestyle totally changes after they finish playing.'

He wasn't joking, but he made me laugh.

Carlton is his own person and has his own views on things, and he will not be swayed or manipulated by others.

I'm also sure that he will be successful in any new ventures he's got planned, because of his strong qualities.

Carlton Palmer and me share a few laughs.

CHAPTER EIGHT
SIR STANLEY MATTHEWS

Stanley Matthews in his playing days.

As you may know, Sir Stan passed away in the year 2000, but I decided to put him in my book. Not just because he was such a great player, but because I had interviewed him myself many years ago.

In the 1977-78 season, I was a professional footballer in Malta, playing for Sliema Wanderers.

Stanley was living in Malta too, in the fishing village of Marsaxlokk, dealing in property and one or two other things.

I acquired his number from the Maltese FA, because he used to coach for the Hibernians, a Maltese team based in the town of Paola.

I spoke to Stanley's secretary, who kindly arranged a meeting in the capital, Valetta.

It turned out that Stanley was the nicest guy in the world. He was very prompt, and very appreciative.

We met in the main square, and then we had lunch in a nice restaurant there. I think it was the Alvine.

We talked for a long time, swapping anecdotes and stories. For a long time afterwards, we kept in touch on the phone. It was a privilege to know him.

⚽

Stanley Matthews was born in Hanley, Stoke on 1 February 1915.

He signed professionally for Stoke City at the age of 17, after joining the club as an office boy aged 15, and joining the reserve team.

Even on the reserve team, Matthews immediately started menacing full-backs with his innovative swerves, and everyone could see that he was going to be a force to be reckoned with.

Stanley's father, Jack Matthews was a local boxer, known as the "Fighting Barber of Hanley". He originally wanted Stan to follow in his footsteps, but Stan only had football on his mind. In 1945, as his father was dying, he made Stanley promise him that he would win the FA Cup.

⚽

As Stanley Matthews got into his stride as a professional at Stoke City, his stature as a footballer was growing week by week, thanks to his sheer brilliance on the wing.

His great dribbling skills were a sight for sore eyes. He didn't use his left foot very much, but once the ball was at his feet, he was just amazing to watch, but frightening to play against.

He missed six good years of professional football with Stoke and England because of World War Two, when he joined the RAF, but he still continued to play throughout the war period with different teams in the Wartime League, and unofficial England International games.

⚽

Stanley Matthews had some glorious years at Stoke, but after being with the club over fifteen years, he thought it was time for a change.

In 1947, he did just that and went to Blackpool for a fee of £11,500.

He had almost left Stoke years earlier, in 1938, disgruntled about a loyalty bonus, but over 3,000 fans organized a special meeting to make it quite clear that they did not want their star player leaving the club. That time, the Stoke City Chairman Albert Booth had also told Matthews that he couldn't leave the club. Eventually all the fuss blew over and Matthews stayed.

In 1947, a new chapter was about to begin for Stanley Matthews at Blackpool, and soon his name would be known all over the world as the great player that he was.

Stan was thirty-two years old when he signed for Blackpool, and most people would think that a player of that age would probably have had his best years already, but not in Stan's case.

The Blackpool manager at that time, Joe Smith, actually asked Matthews if he had many more years left in him.

In fact, fourteen years later, Stan was still at Blackpool, and loving every minute of it.

Matthews did pick up a few injuries along the way but Manager Joe Smith was determined to keep him in the team. Stanley Matthews's chance for glory was just round the corner.

In 1953, Blackpool got to the final of the FA Cup, playing Bolton Wanderers.

The stage was set. What a final it was, with Blackpool coming from behind at 1-3 with only just over thirty minutes left to play. They won 4-3.

Stan had already lost at Wembley twice in two other finals in 1948 and 1951, so it was third time lucky.

Matthews was brilliant, and it's a well-known fact that they called it "The Matthews Final".

At 38 years of age, Stanley Matthews had fulfilled his promise to his father.

It was a great achievement by any standards.

While playing for Blackpool, Matthews was the first footballer to win the Ballon D'Or, the "European Player of the Year" award in 1956, narrowly beating the great Di Stefano of Real Madrid.

Matthews made 440 appearances for Blackpool and scored seventeen goals. He developed a niggling knee injury, and was transferred back to his old club Stoke City in 1961 for a fee of £3,500, which Matthews was not very happy about.

He managed to play in the top division until the grand old age of 50, which is really unbelievable for a player who was kicked from pillar to post, week in week out, while playing with leather balls, on those muddy pitches, in hefty laced-up boots.

It really is remarkable that Matthews could have played that long.

He is also the only player in football history who has received a knighthood while still playing professionally. Stanley's healthy, teetotal lifestyle helped him to maintain his fitness levels for longer than many other footballers.

Matthews' final league game was in 1965, and his total professional appearances at both clubs, including both spells at Stoke totalled 697 games, scoring seventy-one goals.

He did manage to play one more game, at the unbelievable age of 70 years old. He played for an England Veterans team against a Brazilian Veterans team in Brazil which Brazil won 6-1. What a way to finish a glittering career in style!

He won numerous honours whilst he was playing including:

The FA Cup in 1953,
Runners-up in 1948 and 1951 (Blackpool).
Division One Runners-up in 1955-56 (Blackpool).
Division Two Winners in 1932-33, and 1962-63 (Stoke City).
He was voted "Footballer of the Year" in 1948, and 1963.
"European Footballer of the Year" 1956.
He received the CBE in 1957 and a Knighthood in 1965.

❦❀

Stanley Matthews had a brilliant career, and whilst playing for his two clubs, he managed to get fifty-four England caps representing his country, scoring eleven goals.

Probably the most controversial game that he played in was when England played against Germany in Berlin in 1938.

Adolf Hitler was there, watching the game, and the English team were made to stand and make the Nazi salute before the game.

None of the English players wanted to comply, but the British Ambassador ordered them to salute.

England had the last laugh, winning 3-6.

❦☺

As you can see, Sir Stanley Matthews was greatly loved and praised throughout the world, not just in his beloved England.

He was admired from every corner of the globe where football was played.

Sadly, he passed away on 23rd February 2000, at the age of eighty-five years old. More than 100,000 people lined the streets of Stoke to mark their respects at his funeral.

He will be remembered for ever.

In his home town of Hanley, Stoke, a statue of "Sir Stan" has been erected in the town square, and another statue of him stands outside the Britannia stadium, home of Stoke City.

Many professional footballers think that Matthews was the best ever player that graced a football pitch. Others say that he was brilliant at crossing, the master dribbler, and almost anyone who ever met Matthews will tell you what a complete gentleman he was.

❦☺

After he retired from playing, Matthews tried his hand at management, at Port Vale, from 1965-1968. However, he wasn't very successful and unable to get the club out of financial difficulties.

While at Port Vale, Matthews aimed to develop young footballing talent. One success story from Matthews' Port Vale years was a gifted young forward, Mike Cullerton.

I can hardly believe that I played and lived with his brother Bernie Cullerton in Australia with Greek team Pan-Hellenic.

Meanwhile, Stanley Matthews was already travelling the world as an ambassador for football. He coached in various countries but mainly in Africa. In 1975, he defied Apartheid in South Africa to form a team of talented black schoolboys in Soweto, who were known as "Stan's Men".

⚽

In 1977, I was lucky enough to meet the great man.

When I started playing for Maltese Champions, Sliema Wanderers in 1977, I was the only foreign player in Malta at that time.

That's when a friend told me that Stan was living in Malta, and I tracked him down and arranged a meeting with him in Valetta, Malta's capital.

Stanley Matthews was so polite and friendly. When I spoke to him on the phone before we met, I told him my name and that I was an English footballer, playing for Sliema.

He told me that he'd seen me playing for Sliema a few weeks earlier. He remarked that he liked the goal I'd scored. Looking back, I don't know if he was just being polite, but it was great to be complimented by such an icon as Sir Stan.

When we met up, Stanley told me about his training regime.

It was very interesting that for most of his career, all he used to do was to sprint ten yards, there and back, about ten times a day. He would then skip for half an hour or so.

He also told me that he'd became a great dribbler by practicing dribbling around anything in or outside the house. He would dribble around chairs, stools, posts – anything that could test his talents.

Matthews would start his practice sessions slowly, and then gradually speed up. He developed his own rituals in order to succeed at football, and you can see why he excelled.

I will never forget the moment when he said to me:

'Norman – it's a wonderful life being a footballer, getting paid for something you love doing. Always be grateful for having that opportunity.'

Matthews also told me that he didn't touch alcohol and that he'd never smoked, and how against it he really was.

He said that it was impossible for a professional footballer to play to his best ability if he smoked, not even one cigarette a day. He really was very adamant about that.

He also told me that in his entire career, he was never booked or sent off in any game. I found that astounding, considering how many games he played in over the years. A really remarkable achievement.

Stanley Matthews also told me a fascinating story about his footwear. He said that before a game, he would wear his old army boots which were very heavy and cumbersome, and he would walk in them, all the way to the ground.

When he reached the dressing room, he would put his kit on. Only then would he take his army boots off and put on his playing boots.

Immediately, his football boots seemed so much lighter. Psychologically, it made him faster on the pitch.

This technique is very similar to the way a baseball slugger trains. If you pay attention to the hitter, you can see him warming up, swinging two or three heavy practice bats. When he bats with the pitcher for real, his playing bat feels very light in comparison, and he feels like he can hit the ball further.

⚽

Naturally, I had my picture taken with Sir Stan.

Looking back at those photos now brings back great memories, as well as laughter.

I am wearing a pair of flared trousers with dyed black hair, and a moustache. Oh dear! That was 1977, the year of fashion...ha ha!

I remember asking Sir Stan to name his favourite player.

'That's an easy question to answer,' he said. 'Tom Finney was a wonderful player, and Pelé was also beautiful to watch.'

I didn't ask him any other questions about his career, because it wasn't an interview. It was just a present player getting together with an ex-player over a cup of coffee, and sharing each other's stories.

I really loved talking with Sir Stan. He was a complete gentleman: so courteous in every way, and so incredibly humble.

I would have never thought that thirty-seven years later, I would be writing about our meeting in Valetta, Malta.

I am sure that he will never be forgotten: one of the all-time heroes of the great game of football.

All that is left for me to say about him is that I was lucky to have the pleasure of his company for an afternoon in sunny Malta, a long, long time ago, and I shall remember it fondly forever.

Stanley Matthews with me in flares, in 1977.

CHAPTER NINE
DON ROGERS

Don Rogers in the 1970s.

I contacted Don by sending him a letter via Swindon Town Football Club. I asked if he would like to be interviewed for my book, at his convenience of course.

He kindly replied, and said that he was keen to be included in the book.

Don now runs his own well-established sports shop in Swindon, so he's very busy

He told us to come down to see him, and we arranged to come down on a Saturday. He was happy for us to visit, even though it's a busy day for him, because it was the best day for us to drive down. It's a long journey, but we were looking forward to meeting Don.

We had a bit of an adventure driving there and coming back when we took the wrong road, but that's another story!

Don's sports shop is lovely. When we arrived, we called at the back door and knocked at the Indian takeaway next door by mistake, because Don's back door was sealed off.

We had to go in the back of the Indian takeaway and ask if we could go out through his front door to Don's shop. That was a laugh and a half. Luckily, the takeaway staff kindly let us through, and Don was glad to see us.

He courteously offered us a drink right away, and he took us up to the attic of the shop, where it was lovely and quiet. Don, Steve and I sat down and had a lovely chat.

⚽

Don Edward Rogers was born in Paulton, Somerset on 25 October 1945.

He joined Swindon Town FC's youth team in 1961, at the age of fifteen. The youth team reached the cup final, playing against a Manchester United team which featured a teenage George Best. Don told me that even at that young age, he could tell that "Besty" was going to be a little bit special.

Don soon made his first team debut in 1962, aged just sixteen. He played left wing. Don was quick to tell me that a lot of people thought he was left-footed, but actually, he was right-footed.

He explained that he scored lots of goals with his left foot, as well as his right. Unusually, he even scored with both feet when taking penalties, which is an indication of how ambidextrous Don really was.

I wanted to feature Don in my book because I always loved the way he played, being so direct. He loved to run at defenders, whether he was going down the channels or cutting inside.

It didn't matter to Don, because he was such a good dribbler, he could take on defenders on either side.

When I used to watch Don playing, I noticed that he had a very unusual style of running. In fact, he looked like he was hardly moving. However, he was very quick – just ask my brother Maurice.

This is a true story.

I was at home in my lounge with my mates, Steve Conroy, Shaun Rycroft, and my brother Maurice.

We were discussing which footballers I should include in my book.

My brother Maurice is also an ex-professional footballer. After leaving Leeds United, he joined Shrewsbury Town, who were in Division Three at that time.

I said to all three of them:

'I'm thinking of asking Don Rogers to be in it. Do you all remember him?'

Immediately Maurice said: 'Remember him! I had to mark him.'

It was so funny because of the circumstances, and it is surely one of the best "one liners" ever to come out of my brother's mouth, because he didn't mean it to be funny.

Don Rogers is probably not a name that would roll off the tongue like George Best or Jimmy Greaves. However anyone who knows their football would surely remember him.

He had ten good years at Swindon, and will always be remembered for the two extra-time goals that he scored in the 1969 Football League Cup Final at Wembley.

When I asked Don about this game, he told me a story about how things could have turned out.

As most people know, Don was the so-called "hero of the day" for scoring the two goals that won Swindon the Cup in extra-time, but the outcome could have been so different.

When the score was 1-1, Swindon's striker Roger Smart headed the ball against the Arsenal post, and that would have probably been the goal to win the game, but it didn't go in, so the referee blew his whistle for full-time, the game went into extra-time and the rest is history.

Don reflected that if Smart had scored instead of hitting the post, he would have been the Wembley hero instead.

Obviously, that was Don's favourite game ever, and why wouldn't it be, after such a grand finale?

Don gained fame with those two goals in that final, especially the second goal, when he ran from the half-way line to score.

Don laughed about it: 'People love to see players run at people and going around the keepers. I always scored a lot of goals by running around the keepers. It's something I'm remembered for at Swindon.'

He played his last game for Swindon in 1972, and he said he loved every minute of it, scoring 147 goals in 400 appearances, which is remarkably good for a winger.

Don Rogers will always be remembered at The County Ground, for his great presence on the pitch. Swindon Town have re-named the South Stand "The Don Rogers Stand". When a club names a stand after a player, then you know that they were special.

He also said that a lot of people in football thought he should have moved away from Swindon a lot earlier, but Don was very happy there and he really liked the manager, Fred Ford, and the Head Coach, Harry Cousins.

The manager, Fred Ford was a huge guy about six feet four and built like a brick sh*thouse.

'Nobody ever messed with him,' Don said, with a shiver in his voice. 'He was a "no-nonsense" old-school manager.'

One funny story Don told me about Harry Cousins was that one day in training, Don's left boot ripped wide open, so Don asked Harry for some new boots.

Harry came back and gave Don just one left boot. Don say that he always laughs about that because Harry Cousins was so tight-fisted with the kit.

Who was Don's hardest opponent?

'Paul Reaney of Leeds United. He was so hard to get past, because he was so quick.'

In one game, Reaney was marking Don so much in the first half, that they were virtually stuck to each other. Don asked him if he wanted to have a cup of tea with him at half time!

Don also said that Reaney's team mate Paul Madeley was just as fast, and just as hard to get past.

The dirtiest player that Don played against was, without a shadow of doubt, Cardiff City's Dave Carver. He kicked Don every time they played against each other

'He was a real piece of work,' Don said. He once kicked Don on his ankle so hard that the bone was showing through the flesh. Unbelievably, all the trainer did was to tape it up and tell Don to get back on the field.

That's a true story, and Don did go back on until the game was finished. Only then did he receive the proper treatment.

Don didn't hesitate at all when I asked him to name his favourite player:

'George Best. He was so skilful and I loved how he taunted defenders, week after week. He was a fantastic dribbler, and also a great tackler.'

Don always admired his fellow Swindon player, John Trollop, the Swindon full-back.

'He was the fittest player I've ever seen. He could train all day long. He would have been great in today's game, because he was one of the first full-backs to overlap all the time.'

Eventually, Don did move away from Swindon in 1972, and joined Crystal Palace, for a fee of £147,000, with charismatic manager Malcolm Allison in charge.

Don said that Palace did not do very well while he was with the club, but he said that things were going great for him personally. He said that every time he scored, it was on TV.

'Malcolm Allison was a sheer joy to play for because he was a pure football manager. He just loved football so much. He would talk about it all day long. He's definitely the best manager I ever played for.'

Don only played at Palace for two seasons but has great memories to show for it.

He won the "goal of the season" and the "player of the season".

Don scored twice against Manchester United in the league, when Palace thumped United 5-0.

People took more notice of Don at Palace, because he was playing in the top division, and if your team is in that division then you will be on TV every week. If a player is a little bit special (or a lot, in Don's case), then he will get noticed.

In all, Don scored twenty-eight goals in seventy appearances, which is quite good in the top division, considering that he was a wide man.

He played his last game for Crystal Palace in 1974. He told me with a smile on his face that Palace did a swap deal for him, with Queens Park Rangers. Crystal Palace got Terry Venables and John Evans in exchange for Don.

Don commented wryly that at the time, he had a knackered hip, Venables had a knackered knee and Evans had a knackered ankle.

'All three of us were ready for the knacker's yard!'

However, Don played for Queens Park Rangers from 1974 until 1976, appearing in eighteen matches and scoring five goals.

He then returned to Swindon in 1976, for his second time at the club, but only stayed for a season, scoring two goals in twelve games.

Don decided to call it a day, and played his last game in 1977, before retiring.

He now runs his own sports shop near the ground, and has been there for over forty years.

While at Swindon Town, Don played for the England under 23s and also for the Football League Team, but he never got a full England call-up.

One thing Don told me that I found interesting was that he'd never read a contract in his entire career. He'd just signed it and that was that.

I asked him what he thought about football nowadays.

'There are too many racist allegations flying around like confetti. It's a distraction from just playing the game, and has become over the top.'

Don doesn't like the so-called cheats who dive in the box all the time. He says it's too much now, because everyone is doing it.

'It started with foreign players, but now they all do it. I think that anyone who does that should be suspended by the FA'

I totally agree with him because it's time it was stopped.

Don doesn't have too much to do with football nowadays, apart from watching Swindon's home games in the Directors box and his free car parking ticket.

I asked Don about his favourite memory.

'Getting married to my lovely wife,' he said. I thought that was rather sweet.

I'm so glad that I took the long journey there and back to Swindon to meet Don, because he was a real gentleman, full of humour and great stories.

He was an absolute pleasure to be with and I loved every minute of his company.

Trophy cabinet: with Don Rogers in his sports shop.

CHAPTER TEN
ARCHIE GEMMILL

Archie Gemmill at the World Cup in 1978.

I contacted Derby County, and spoke to their lovely secretary, Sarah.

She gave me Archie's address and phone number, and told me that he was keen on being interviewed for the book at some point in the future.

Soon afterwards, on a Bank Holiday, we were driving past Chesterfield, and we realised that we were passing very near to Archie Gemmill's house and we may as well just knock on his door! His house was just outside Derby.

We hoped that he wouldn't be too mad with us, as he had agreed to the interview. We had been trying to call him, with no success, and I said it was worth a try. The worst thing that could happen was that he turned us away at the door.

We found his house, and I knocked at the door, and Archie himself answered it. I introduced myself and told him why I'd called. He was rather surprised at me appearing on his doorstep.

I apologised about "cold calling", but I explained that I had been trying to get in touch with him and I was keen to get him into the book.

Archie apologised: he said that he'd been abroad and had been really busy, and that he had to go to Scotland, but that an interview would be okay in the future.

I cheekily said: 'while we're here, could you give us ten minutes of your time?'

Archie said that he was on his way out, but I put on my best charm and told him that we wanted him in the book because he was such a great player. Very kindly, he agreed to it then and there.

'Come around the back,' he said. 'We'll make it quick.'

The house was a really pretty old farmhouse, and we talked in the conservatory. Archie warmed up when we started interviewing him, and we took a few good pictures.

We needed to interview him, and he just needed a little persuasion. The old charm's still there!

⚽

Archibald "Archie" Gemmill was born in Paisley, Scotland on 24 March 1947.

In 1964, he joined his first club in the Scottish League, St. Mirren, but he was plagued with injuries, including a broken ankle.

He was also the first Scotsman to be used as a tactical substitute in 1966, when he was brought on in a Scottish League Cup game.

In 1967, Archie transferred to an English club, Preston North End, for £13,000. He was soon noticed by the keen eye of Peter Taylor, one half of the legendary management "double act" with Brian Clough at Derby County.

⚽

Cloughie knew that Gemmill would be a great signing for Derby County. He loved Archie's high energy and passing ability, and he was determined to get his man.

The story goes that when Gemmill refused to sign for Derby County, Cloughie told him that he would not drive back home until Archie signed for the club. Cloughie said that he would sleep outside Archie's house in his car all night if he had to.

Archie's wife asked him to come inside and stay the night, and the following morning, Archie Gemmill was a Derby County player, signed for £60,000 in 1970.

He won the football league title twice with Derby County, in 1971/73, and 1974/75, and the FA Charity Shield in 1975, making 261 appearances and scoring seventeen goals.

Archie told me that he loved playing at Derby, because of the obvious success he had there, and the great players alongside him.

However, one thing he hated was the pitch at Derby, the Baseball Ground.

'It was absolutely shocking. It was a mud heap, even more after a little rain. Once the groundsman told us: "Enjoy playing on it, lads, because this is a good surface today." It was about six inches deep in thick mud.'

⚽

Brian Clough moved from Derby County to their close neighbours Nottingham Forest, and he quickly made up his mind that he wanted the nucleus of the Derby midfield to come with him, which included Archie. As a result, Archie transferred to Forest for £25,000 in 1977.

At Forest, Archie Gemmill won the football league title again for the third time, in 1977/78, and the Football League Cup, in 1978 and in 1979.

Forest also won the very prestigious European Cup in 1979, but surprisingly Archie was dropped from the line-up, and he was said to have been "sick as a pig" not to have played in the final.

In all, Archie played a total of fifty-eight games for Forest and scored just four goals. Being dropped for the European

Cup Final did not lie well with Archie and it marked the beginning of the end for his Nottingham Forest career. He left the club in 1979, signing for Birmingham City, where he played ninety-seven times, scoring twelve goals.

Archie stayed at Birmingham for three years, and then in 1982, he moved "over the pond", to play in the USA for the Jacksonville Tea Men in the NASL League.

One season was enough for him, and after playing just thirty-two games and scoring two goals, he returned home. In the same year, he signed for Wigan Athletic. The club was managed at the time by Archie's old team mate Larry Lloyd. Archie played just eleven games for Wigan Athletic.

Archie's final team signing was for his old club Derby County, for his old boss and mentor, Peter Taylor, where he played sixty-three games and scored eight goals.

Archie finally hung up his boots in 1984.

⚽

Archie Gemmill found astounding success with Derby County and Nottingham Forest, but he will always be remembered for the great goal he scored for Scotland against Holland in the 1978 World Cup.

As a player, he was not renowned for scoring many goals, but his goal against Holland had "special" written all over it.

I asked Archie about the goal, and he said that even today, people are always asking him about it.

He was very pleased that his goal had given so many people such pleasure, and it showed in his expression when he told me.

I think the most famous reference to it is in the cult film *Trainspotting*, where the character Renton, played by the actor Ewan McGregor, is having sex with his girlfriend. After he climaxes, he says: 'Phew! I haven't felt that good since Archie Gemmill scored against Holland in 1978!'

Archie told me that a picture of him scoring the goal was featured on the front of a well-known credit card.

He was very happy to talk about that famous goal, and I don't blame him either. It's widely known as one of the greatest ever World Cup goals.

⚽

Archie played forty-three times for Scotland, scoring eight goals in total, from 1971 to 1981. He was the team captain for twenty-two of those games.

'I really loved playing for my country,' he told me.

Archie also coached the Scotland under-nineteens team from 2005 until 2009.

In 1970, when Archie's wife was pregnant and about to go into labour, he drove her all the way back to Scotland, just so that his son Scot, would be born there and so be eligible to play for the Scottish team! It paid off, as Scot did play for Scotland when he grew up.

≈ ⊛

After Archie's playing career finished, he came up North to my neck of the woods, as we say here in good old Yorkshire.

He became manager of little Rotherham United, from 1994 until 1996, and took them to Wembley in his last season, for the first time in the club's history, to win the Football League Trophy Final.

I asked Archie what he thought about the game today. He told me that he thinks the game is much better developed these days, with training methods and specialised diets for the players.

We also talked about the pitches of today, and Archie agreed with Ron Atkinson's comments to me.

'Players like George Best would be world beaters, playing old these plush surfaces nowadays – not like the muddy old Baseball Ground.'

Archie told me that he would have loved to have seen gifted players like Stanley Matthews and Tom Finney play on these lovely pitches. He thinks they would have been great to watch.

Archie hates the way that big money is ruining the game, and how a lot of the big clubs are being taken over by overseas directors and foreign signings.

We got talking about the great football players of today. He thinks that Ronaldo is better than Messi, which a lot of people will agree with, but a lot will disagree.

Archie told me without hesitation that his favourite all-time player is Pelé.

His ever hardest opponent was the tenacious and brilliant Billy Bremner.

Archie's favourite football match was a game his son Scot played in, while he was with Nottingham Forest. It was the football League Cup, and Nottingham Forest were playing against Southampton. Forest won 3-2 and Scot Gemmill scored twice.

⚽☺

Well, certainly Archie Gemmill was a footballer who is remembered by some people for his ability, and by others for giving pleasure to Ewan McGregor in a well-known movie!

Acting tough in Archie's conservatory.

CHAPTER ELEVEN
NEIL WARNOCK

Neil Warnock playing for Barnsley in 1977.

I didn't think that Neil would be too hard to meet up with. He's been a friend of mine for years. We played together at Chesterfield, when we were both young lads.

We've kept in touch over the years, so I already had Neil's number. I gave him a call to see if he wanted to be in the book.

When I was living in the Philippines back in 2001, I called Neil at Sheffield United, to tell him about a young Filipino player, Ryan Payson. I'd been coaching him and he was a brilliant young talent.

Neil was impressed and we tried to get Ryan to Sheffield for a month's trial. Unfortunately, we kept hitting red tape with visa problems, and so unfortunately we never got the trial off the ground.

Neil lives in Cornwall, and when we arranged the interview, he'd left his last club, Leeds United, and he wasn't coaching any more.

He suggested that I meet him down at Talksport, the radio station where Neil does a regular show. The studios are in the middle of London.

I told Neil: 'No problem, that's fine! Me and Steve will meet you down there!'

We had a horrendous journey into the centre of London. There were no problems getting to the outskirts of London in our car and parking at the station. We got there at seven o'clock, so we could catch Neil's show in the studio. He was on air until ten o' clock, co-presenting with another ex-footballer, Alan Brazil.

We took the Tube. It was twenty-odd pounds for a journey of about twelve stops. The carriage was ridiculously packed from pillar to post: a full-on rush hour. Believe me, it really was rush hour! We noticed that everyone apart from us was wearing headphones. I'd never seen anything like it. It was pandemonium!

We got off the Tube at Waterloo station and realized that we were lost. We asked a stranger for directions. He looked up the address on his i-phone, and we found out that the Talksport offices were only a five minute walk away.

It was weird. We walked down a busy street, and there it was – a five-a-side football pitch, right in the middle of London, on the main road outside Talksport, in between houses and businesses. The staff probably played five-a-side at lunchtime.

It reminded me of the De La Salle team's pitch at Manila University, where I had coached, amongst all the buildings, with no grass anywhere else.

We went inside Talksport, and spoke to a young secretary. I asked for Neil Warnock.

'Hello, you must be Norman,' she replied, in a very sexy, sultry voice.

'Yes, that's me,' I said.

'Just wait here, please,'

She offered us a cup of tea, and we sat down in the reception. Neil and Alan were on air. We could see them broadcasting via a TV monitor above our sofa.

I was very impressed with Talksport, and I can see why it's very popular.

❦❀

Neil Warnock was born in Sheffield, South Yorkshire, on 1 December, 1948.

Neil started his football career at Chesterfield in 1967. I was playing for Chesterfield at that time too, and Neil and I became friends soon after we met, probably because we were both from Sheffield.

Neil was an out and out winger:

'I was quick, but I never had a brain,' he told me, which really made me laugh.

Neil complimented me, and said that I had a good footballing brain, but that I had other things on my mind to distract me. I wonder what he meant?

Neil was at Chesterfield for two years, and enjoyed himself there, appearing in twenty-four games and scoring two goals. He told me later that Chesterfield was probably his favourite club, out of all the teams he'd played for.

Neil remembers playing away for Chesterfield at Luton Town. Malcolm Macdonald, "Supermac", played left-back that day for Luton. He was marking Neil too close for comfort. He left his mark too, scarring Neil down his right leg.

⚽

In 1969, he left Chesterfield and joined their old local rivals Rotherham United. He played there until 1971, making fifty two appearances and scoring five goals.

He then moved on again to Hartlepool United, playing there until 1973, making sixty appearances and scoring five goals.

Neil was voted "Player of the Year" at Hartlepool in 1972. When he received his trophy, he was told that he would have to give it back after one year, and they would replace it with a replica trophy.

'Norm, this is no word of a lie,' Neil laughed. 'I kept writing to them for over twenty years, and eventually I got my replica in 1998. I waited twenty-six years for it!'

As Neil told this story in the Talksport offices, I'm sure that everyone could hear us, we were laughing so loud!

❦❀

In 1973, Neil packed his bags again and moved to Scunthorpe United, staying there for two seasons, playing in seventy-two games and scoring seven goals.

Then in 1975, he moved again to Aldershot, where he appeared in thirty-seven games and scored six goals. Ever the wanderer, in 1976, he packed his suitcase again and moved to Barnsley.

❦❀

Neil had a great season in Barnsley in 1977. That year, Neil scored ten goals, his highest of any season with any team.

'It was just a great year for me,' Neil said. 'I played well, made lots of assists, and my goal-scoring was in double figures for the first time in my career.'

Neil really enjoyed his time with the "Tykes" and left in 1978, with fifty-seven appearances under his belt.

Next club in line for Neil was York City, where my uncle Arthur Bottom had been a top goal scorer in the mid-1950s.

Neil only played four games for the club, without scoring a goal, and the same year, he quickly moved on to his last club, Crewe Alexandra.

Neil played at Crewe until 1979, finishing his playing career after twenty-one games and scoring just one goal for the club.

Neil certainly did his share of travelling. Personally, I think that's the best route, but others will say that it's always best to stay with one or two clubs throughout your career.

I think it depends on the individual player, and what they're naturally suited to.

Neil played his football in different towns and cities in England, whereas I played my football in different countries around the world.

Neil only waited a year before he got back into the game, but not as a player this time. He started his managerial career, which was destined to have many twists and turns.

He started with non-league Gainsborough Trinity, and soon after, managed Burton Albion.

Then he moved to Scarborough.

'That was one of my greatest achievements,' he told me.

What Neil did at Scarborough was amazing.

When he took over the Manager's job in 1986, Scarborough only had two players registered on their books, so Neil set up trials for forty-two unknown players that summer, before the new season started. In the end, he signed up seventeen players from the trials.

By the end of September, Scarborough were at the bottom of the Conference League.

The Scarborough Chairman was quoted in the all the national papers, saying that it was the worst Scarborough team that he had ever seen.

Things looked bad.

However, in that same month, Neil signed goalkeeper Kevin Blackwell, and Scarborough went on an incredible run throughout the rest of the season, without losing a game.

They won the title, and Scarborough were promoted into the football league, making them the first team to win automatic promotion from the Conference League.

Unbelievably, the bookmakers had put the odds on Scarborough getting promoted at 50/1. I wish I'd put £100 quid on that.

Neil stayed at Scarborough until 1989, and then moved on to Notts County, where once again, he had great success, achieving two promotions back-to-back.

He got Notts County promoted into Division Two, and the next year into Division One.

Neil said that those two promotions gave him a lot of satisfaction, and that he loved managing the team.

He stayed with Notts County until 1993. While he was there, he nurtured a lot of new talent.

Neil developed one of the most talented centre-backs he'd ever worked with, Craig Shaw. Neil took him from his job as a bank clerk and turned him into a brilliant defender. Neil also said that Craig was a great prospect for England at that time.

✿

Neil left Notts County for a very brief spell at Torquay United.

He soon moved onto Huddersfield Town, in the same season. Once again, the "Warnock Magic" struck again, getting Huddersfield promoted. Neil stayed there until 1995.

Neil wasn't finished yet, moving on to Plymouth Argyle, where once again, he got his team promoted to Division Two.

He moved onto new pastures in 1997, to Oldham Athletic. Neil stayed just a season. In 1998, he moved to Bury, but he didn't stay there long, leaving in 1999.

Bigger clubs were now taking notice of Neil's achievements as a manager. You have to give the man credit. He did very well, considering he never had any money for players in the clubs that he managed early in his management career.

I've known Neil for over forty-five years, even though we lost touch occasionally, mainly due to me playing or coaching abroad. I never had any doubts about Neil's success in management at any level of football, because he's a born winner.

In 1999, Neil's dream job came along.

That could have only been one club: Sheffield United.

Neil has always been a "Blade", as long as I've known him, so you can imagine what he must have felt when he was offered the job to manage the team he'd followed since boyhood.

'I used to go to Bramall Lane and watch my heroes – Jimmy Hagan, Joe Shaw, and half-back Brian Richardson. He was amazing.'

Neil confessed that United only offered him the job because the team had no money and couldn't afford anyone who had any stature in the game.

The great Derek Dooley interviewed Neil. A hero for Sheffield Wednesday fans from the 1950s, he was now the Managing Director of their rival club.

Derek asked Neil what his ambitions were for United.

'I want this club to be the best in Sheffield, the best in Yorkshire, take them to Wembley, and get promoted to the Premier League,' Neil said.

Derek was impressed.

So was Neil. Derek Dooley was the greatest person Neil had ever met in football. He admired him so much.

Neil also admitted that Sheffield Wednesday (my team), were a much bigger club, with a much bigger history, and he was determined to turn that round.

He did just that.

When Neil took over at "The Lane", the crowd attendances were around 8,000 a game, but when he left, the gates had tripled to around 25,000, which once again was a wonderful achievement.

He took the team to Wembley three times, once in the League Cup semi-final, and again in the FA Cup semi-final.

The third Wembley visit was in the play-off final. It was the first time that Neil had experienced a loss in the play-offs, after winning four on the bounce.

Neil really enjoyed himself at United but who wouldn't, in the same position? He was in his element, managing the team he'd followed since childhood.

Neil's greatest achievement ever in football was getting United promoted to the Premier League in the 2005-6 season.

He revelled in it and I didn't blame him one bit. It must have been a great day in his life.

❦⊛

The glory wasn't going to last. By the end of the next season, Sheffield United were fighting against relegation. The team seemed to be surviving, but fate was due to play its hand.

The fatal turning point came when West Ham beat Manchester United 1-0 on the last day of the season. The goal was scored by Argentinian player Carlos Tevez, whose contract with West Ham was in question over third party ownership issues. Tevez wasn't fully under contract, and West Ham were later fined £5.5 million pounds by the Premier League for letting Tevez play in the match.

Meanwhile, at Bramall Lane, Sheffield United were playing Wigan, with a score of 1-1, but a penalty was awarded to Wigan in injury time at the end of the first half. Ironically, an ex-blade, David Unsworth, scored the penalty.

Sheffield United were relegated to the Championship League, in what became known at the "Tevez incident".

Following the "Tevez incident", Sheffield United appealed to be reinstated to the Premier League. When this appeal was unsuccessful, they accepted a financial settlement of £20 million.

Although Sheffield United's relegation was completely out of Warnock's control, they didn't give him the "staying-up" bonus they had promised.

Neil felt let down by the club, and the good times were over.

⚽

Neil blamed himself for one thing: letting a small minority of fans, approximately three hundred of them, get under his skin.

They were constantly chanting for Neil to be sacked.

He came out with a very insightful statement:

'The majority of fans were happy with me. They just let things ride along from game to game. Only the unhappy minority make a fuss.'

The disgruntled fans succeeded in getting Neil to resign, when he should have been thinking positively. Thousands of fans were more than happy with him.

I should know. I've been there myself. The same thing happened to me in Australia; the only difference being was that I was a player, and not a manager like Neil.

Chris Morgan, Sheffield United's captain at the time, told Neil not to go, and not to listen to the three hundred idiots chanting him out.

Neil just thought to himself:

'Be careful what you wish for.'

Neil told me that his favourite player from the teams he'd managed was Michael Brown.

Brown scored twenty-three goals in the season Sheffield United were promoted to the Premier League.

'Michael Brown was a so-called "bad-boy" when he was at Manchester City, but I managed to turn him around,' Neil said. 'I was rewarded for my patience.'

I asked Neil to name his favourite player of all-time.

'George Best. There was no one better than Georgie-boy.'

Neil said that he would have loved to have played with Sheffield United, but he admitted that he just wasn't good enough.

Nearly all of his finest hours in football were when he was managing United.

'My favourite game of all time has to be one of the Sheffield derbies.'

'Which one?' I asked.

'Any of them!' Neil chuckled.

After leaving Sheffield United, Neil Warnock joined Crystal Palace in 2007.

He did rather well in his first year with Palace, and in the space of a few months, he turned them around.

At the start of the season, they were near the bottom of the league, but by the spring, they were challenging for a play-off place. Unfortunately, they lost in the semi-finals.

Despite the club's worsening financial situation, Warnock did well there.

He left Crystal Palace in 2010, as the club were placed into Administration.

⟪❂⟫

Neil's next managerial move was to Palace's neighbours, Queens Park Rangers.

Neil quickly got down to business and prevented QPR from relegation in his first season at the club.

His next season was a totally different story.

The team started the new season in the Championship League, with hard work and flair from key players like Adel Taarabt.

Neil told me that he made Taarabt team captain, so he could get him to play even better. It paid off, because Warnock got an extra 20% out of the Moroccan player.

However, later, Neil told Taarabt that he would never play like that again, because other managers would not put up with his temperamental outbursts. Having Taarabt on the team was a "luxury". He had amazing potential, but had to be pushed to live up to it, which is probably why Harry Redknapp got rid of him at Tottenham.

Neil told me that it was the first time in his managerial career that he had built a team around one player. His teams were known for working hard, with lots of team spirit.

'By making Taarabt the team captain, QPR got promoted,' Neil reflected. Queens Park Rangers were promoted into the Premiership in April 2011, after beating Watford 2-0.

Neil did a fantastic job getting QPR in the Premiership, but he paid the price for a run of bad results, and was sadly sacked, for the first time, in a management career of almost fifteen years.

Neil told me that there was no justification behind his sacking, which happened after QPR lost 1-2 to Norwich City on 2nd January 2012.

The sad thing was that in their promotion year, Queens Park Rangers had already won the title by April. Then they made the mistake of not buying any new players, so they weren't ready for the new season in the Premier league.

The reason that the team didn't buy any new players was that the owners were selling the club. No players were bought until August, a week before the season started. They actually signed five players on deadline day.

The season started badly, as expected, and it continued that way, with Neil paying the price in 2012, losing his job half way through the season.

➄◉

Neil did not have long to wait until he was back in the dugout. In the same year, his old pal Ken Bates offered him the manager's job at Leeds United.

'It was a similar situation to QPR,' Neil explained. 'Bates wanted to sell the club, and I tried to help him out.'

Neil told me that Leeds United would have been a decent team, if they had just bought two players with pace. He really believes that that's all it would have taken to turn Leeds into a good team.

Installed as manager, Warnock got rid of a lot of "dead wood", as he calls it. With a bit of time and a few new signings, he's sure that he could have turned the team around in a relatively short time.

Neil only took the job because his son James, who lives in Leeds, kept bugging him about becoming the team's manager. However, Neil admitted to me that he spent more time trying to sell the club than actually coaching.

Neil only wanted to be at Leeds in the short term anyway, because it was too far from the rest of his family.

He told me that he got on fairly well with Ken Bates, but that he was very hard to work with as the team's manager.

Just before he took the Leeds job, Neil told me that he was lined up for the manager's job at Wolverhampton. If he'd have waited for three days, he would have taken the "Wolves" job, and he honestly thinks that he would have stopped them from being relegated.

Neil left Leeds on the 1st April 2013.

⚽

I asked Neil if he had another club lined up in the very near future. He just said:

'Well, Norm, to be quite honest, I've had thirty-three years now as a manager. I just can't get that excited anymore about being on the touchline in the wind and rain.'

He reflected that he had been sadly let down by different clubs, which had disillusioned him to a point that he just didn't give a damn any more.

Having said that, he hinted to me that there was one club that he would be interested in. He was keeping his cards close to his chest, and wouldn't tell me which club he had in mind.

'If the deal's right, I'd take it. But the club would have to agree to my conditions.'

'Neil. Never say never,' I said.

It's easy to see why Neil didn't feel in a hurry to be a manager again.

❦

I asked Neil for his opinions on the footballers of today.

He thinks that there's a total lack of respect in the game these days.

'The players don't have any time for anyone but themselves. They don't sign autographs anymore.'

Neil feels that money has spoilt the game too much and that all the old characteristics of the game are rapidly disappearing.

Obviously, I brought up the topic of Neil managing my much loved Sheffield Wednesday, and he was keen to do it, but in December 2013 when he was in the running for the job, a few bigoted "Owls" fans had protested against Neil taking the job because he's a "Blade" through and through.

Who cares? I certainly didn't, because at that time he was the right man for the job, with no one else available coming close to Neil's credentials. I know he has slagged off Wednesday in the past, but he was with United at the time so what do you expect from him? At the end of the day, it was just a little bit of banter.

Neil told me that the Sheffield Wednesday Chairman Milan Mandarić offered him the job, and Neil really and sincerely wanted to help keep Wednesday in the Championship.

However, he made it clear that he would only have managed the team for a few months, just to help out.

Neil totally agrees with me that it is a crying shame that a city the size of Sheffield doesn't have both its teams in the Premiership.

Neil's his exact words were: 'It's a f*cking joke.'

I remember Neil being offered the Chelsea job many years ago, back in the 90s. However, he said he couldn't do the dirty on Notts County, and the players all pleaded with him to stay with the club.

Neil admitted that at that time, he was a little bit scared of living in London, and that was also one of the reasons why he didn't take the job.

Nowadays, he loves London and thinks that it's a fascinating city.

Neil really loved being in the Premier League as a manager, and he looks back most fondly on his time at Sheffield United. However, he also agrees with me and thinks that there is too much money available for foreign players, and as a result, the football clubs are failing to nurture home-grown talent. Our

England team is suffering and will continue to suffer in the future.

Neil is very happy living in Cornwall with his family. He really loves it down there, and he commutes to London to work for Talksport radio station, every Monday from 6-10 am on the Alan Brazil show, talking live to fans who call in asking questions and debating certain aspects of the game.

Neil loves broadcasting, and has just signed a new two-year contract with BT as a football pundit. He's very excited about it, but says that he's got to be very careful – he's now working more hours than he did as a manager, and he doesn't want to overstretch himself.

I asked Neil if he could remember my stint as a football commentator for the BBC, on Radio Sheffield back in the 80s.

I only did it for a short while, because I had recently returned from playing abroad. Bob Jackson gave me the start I needed. His "Praise or Grumble" show was the first ever football phone-in. I wish I'd kept it up, because I did enjoy commentating very much.

When Neil goes to Talksport, he often gets taxi drivers asking him to come to Millwall and help them out! He says they all love him down there and are always barracking him to take the Millwall job.

Well, it was always going to be interesting to interview my old mate Neil, and he didn't disappoint.

I'm sure that Mr. Warnock will be turning up on our television screens sooner or later in the very near future. Neil is certainly one of the games' most enduring characters, and the world of football is sadly lacking in people like Neil. He is a true "one-off".

Two old buddies having a moment!

CHAPTER TWELVE
DAVID HIRST

David Hirst in his 90s
Sheffield Wednesday strip.

I got David's number from my old pal Mel Sterland, who is his ex-team-mate at Sheffield Wednesday. Mel said:

'David likes a crack, and he likes what you're doing. He'll be up for an interview.'

As I told you earlier, we arranged to meet in the wine bar in the basement of the Beauchief Hotel, where I also met Carlton Palmer. You could say that our meeting went very smoothly indeed!

❦☉

David Eric Hirst was born in Cudworth, Barnsley on 7 December 1967. He joined Barnsley in 1985 and scored nine goals in twenty-eight appearances in his first season of professional football.

Watching his progress religiously was Howard Wilkinson, the Sheffield Wednesday Manager. He bought Hirst, by then nicknamed "The Cudworth Flyer" for £250,000 in 1986.

Hirst was an instant hit with the Owls' fans, as they liked his "Gung-Ho" style and attitude, and he went on to be a real favourite with the fans, scoring 106 goals in 294 appearances.

David Hirst played in three finals with Sheffield Wednesday. In 1993, he played and scored against Arsenal in the FA Cup Final, which Arsenal won after a replay, and in the same year, he faced Arsenal again in the Football League Cup Final, which Arsenal also won.

However David got a Winners' Medal in 1991, when the Owls beat Manchester United in the Football League Cup final. In that match, Sheffield Wednesday player John Sheridan scored the only goal of the game. Ironically, he was a Manchester United fan.

◌

After eleven good years at Hillsborough, David Hirst moved down south to join Southampton for £2,000 000.

He played there for three seasons, but after numerous injuries, he decided to call it a day on medical advice, and played his last game in 2000.

He retired from playing football at the age of thirty-two.

A lot of people think that David Hirst never fully recovered after a match in 1992 at Arsenal, when Steve Bould tackled him and left Hirst with a broken ankle.

Hirst also played for England three times, but would have surely had more caps if he hadn't been injured so much.

🏃⚽

When I interviewed David, I could tell right away that it was going to be a classic meeting with another classic footballer.

He was very forthcoming, and did not take himself too seriously at all.

I must admit that for some strange reason, I didn't think he would be as jovial as he was. Perhaps I thought he'd be reserved, because of his quiet presence on the field, but in fact he had me laughing for almost two hours, with some great one-liners.

David had some brilliant stories. I can't reveal all of them here, but I can tell you that he doesn't suffer fools at all.

He doesn't like people who are full of crap, and he tells it how it is – just like me, so I knew that we would get along just fine.

Not only did David score goals, but he told me that one time when he was playing for Sheffield Wednesday against Manchester City, the Owls' keeper Kevin Pressman was injured, and so David went in goal.

Wednesday won 2-0 and David kept a clean sheet, as well as scoring before he went in goal.

How's that? I cannot remember anyone else achieving that double feat.

If any of you fans out there know of someone else who has done that, please let me know!

I didn't know that he'd played in goal for Wednesday, because the game was back in 1990, and I was still playing in Texas at that time.

⚽

Another story about Hirsty that not many people know is that for over a decade, he held the record for the "Hardest Shot" recorded.

When people talk about players who had a very hard shot, they always think of ex-Leeds United player Peter Lorimer, but believe it or not, he wasn't even in the top ten lists.

In 1996, Sheffield Wednesday played Arsenal at Highbury, and Hirst hit the bar at 114 mph, which was only beaten by a Portuguese player called Ronny in 2006.

⚽

I asked David what he was doing now for a living, and he told me that he has just started working with the Sheffield

Wednesday Academy, coaching the young players, and some of the older ones too.

Dean Ramsdale, the Academy Director, has asked David to come down to Sheffield Wednesday to give some inspiration and pass on some useful knowledge to the younger players.

David is also working with the strikers at the academy, showing them how not to be predictable in their play, and how to change their game from time to time.

Let's face, it David's knowledge on how to play upfront is second to none, so I'm sure that he will be a big success with the youngsters and youth players.

David told me that a lot of the younger players of today don't have the same attitude towards making the grade as they did twenty years ago. I totally agree with him.

Young footballers don't seem as driven to succeed as we were in our day.

In my opinion, kids now have too much of everything; computers, Xboxes, and mobile phones.

All I had when I was a kid was a Frido plastic ball that cost about fifty pence in today's money, and thirty of us would play from morning until night at the weekends, only stopping for lunch and dinner, and playing almost every night after we finished school.

⚽

David has been coaching at the Academy now for about six months. He told me that he's really enjoying it. He wanted to get back in the game, and hopefully, it's a good stepping stone for future things.

He told me that he didn't really want to get into coaching after he finished playing in 2000. He had the time to enjoy watching his kids grow up. Now that they're older, he has the time to do something, and the opportunity came just at the right time for him.

I confessed to David that it can sometimes be a nightmare coaching young kids, because they want to do what they want, and their concentration level is minimal, to say the least.

I have coached all over the world, on five different continents. The worst kids to coach are definitely the ones in the USA.

They are totally spoilt little brats and every parent, and I do mean every, thinks that their kid is the best player in the team.

When it came to Saturdays, when we played our games, and I could only start eleven kids out of a squad of sixteen, you can imagine the constant earache that I would get from the parents. They'd be moaning for the whole morning if I didn't pick their kid to start.

It was the same from the under sevens to the under nineteens in both boys' and girls' teams.

When I was living in Washington D.C., it was an especially stressful time, because most of the parents were in the military or in politics, and they thought they knew everything.

It was also bad in Texas, where I spent almost ten years, but the parents there were marginally more laid back!

⚽

David says that he sometimes does after dinner speaking, and let me tell you all, that if you have a chance to hear him tell his old football tales, then go and listen, because I for one found him very entertaining throughout. He is a very funny person – the kind I love to interview.

David loves coaching and the dinner dates, and I am sure he will go far, now he's back in the footballing world, with his beloved Sheffield Wednesday.

I'm certain that David will be a very good role model because of how he used to play the game. He had all the attributes that a top striker needs: strength, great pace, and a keen eye for scoring goals.

He was also an honest player, not a so-called "diver", as so many of them are these days. I must confess that I get sick and tired of watching the strikers of today go down at the slightest of touches and then reel over and over again.

Unfortunately, David was plagued by genuine injuries. That broken ankle from Steve Bould's notorious challenge in 1992

148

seemed to start a chain of further injuries that prevented Hirst from stardom on the England team.

‹›

I asked David if he had any regrets.

'Yes – f*cking thousands!' he said. He started laughing.

One question I had to ask was about the time when Sir Alex Ferguson wanted to take him to Manchester United.

Did he regret not going there?

David looked at me.

'Just go to the bottom of my driveway at home, and you will see a suitcase with a tag on saying "Old Trafford this way".' I laughed my b*ll*cks off when David said this. 'There's also another suitcase at my mum's house in Cudworth, just in case the first one goes missing.'

Sir Alex Ferguson tried numerous times to buy David Hirst, but Wednesday would not let their prize possession leave, and so Sir Alex bought Eric Cantana instead, and the rest is history.

One thing that David really misses is the camaraderie with his old Hillsborough mates.

'Sometimes fourteen or fifteen players would all go out for a meal and a laugh. These days, it just doesn't happen. Nobody wants to do anything anymore. They just want to leave and do their own thing,' he said. 'It was great when I was playing, because everybody looked out for each other. It bonded the team on and off the field, but not anymore.'

❦☺

David's favourite goal was scoring in the Cup Final against Arsenal.

'Every striker wants to score in the final,' he said. 'I'll always treasure that memory.'

The favourite club that David played for is obviously Sheffield Wednesday.

Without any hesitation, David told me that his favourite manager is "Big Ron" Atkinson.

David could not be pinned down to pick the favourite game that he'd ever played in. Not even the final in which he scored.

'Norm, you can't pick a game just because you score in it, because you have to win the game too.' David mentioned numerous games, but there wasn't one that stood out above the rest, so I let that question slide.

David had several "hardest opponents":

'All the Arsenal defenders – Steve Adams, Steve Bould, and Lee Dixon in particular, always gave me a hard time.'

I left it until last to ask David about his favourite player of all time.

'Glenn Hoddle,' he said. Not a bad choice at all. I liked his silky skills too.

I was pleased to hear David tell me that he was never greedy about his earnings, and he said that he'd never knocked on a manager's door for a pay rise.

David was never bothered about how much other players were earning. He said that he didn't give a damn if they were earning more or less than him. He was just happy to be playing and getting paid.

I believe David 100%. Every word was true and sincere.

The thing that really made me warm to David in a big way was when I asked him why he hadn't written his autobiography.

'Norm, I would never write a book. Because in the past, I have seen other players do just that and fill the book with rubbish. Also I might mention something that could incriminate somebody who I know, and I wouldn't do that, just to earn a few bob from my book sales.'

That, my dear friends, is a man of integrity. Something that you don't see very often in the sporting world.

I must say that I really enjoyed watching David Hirst play, and now can proudly say that I also enjoy his company.

A true meeting of minds with David Hirst.

CHAPTER THIRTEEN
FRANK WORTHINGTON

Frank Worthington: with classic 70s flowing locks.

To contact Frank Worthington, I sent an email and a letter to Leicester City. Their secretary, Geoff, sent me a helpful reply, saying that he would pass my details onto Frank.

I was at home a few weeks later when the phone rang.

'Hello? Is that Norman Parkin? This is Frank Worthington.' He had a very pleasant voice.

Frank told me that he'd love to meet me and that he liked my idea of putting a book together to help people affected by the typhoon in the Philippines.

'I love your handwriting!' he said, which embarrassed me a bit.

We couldn't work out the best place to meet at first. We were going to meet in Huddersfield, then Halifax, and then we decided to think about it, because Frank's wife organises his schedule.

I called him back a few days later, and we agreed to meet just off the M62, at the Cedar Court, a lovely hotel, on Saturday lunchtime.

Well, as luck would have it, Wigan Athletic Football Club were playing Huddersfield that very same day, and the players were staying in the hotel!

As we were doing the interview, the team arrived at the hotel for their pre-match meal. The new German manager of Wigan, Ywe Röslar came over to talk to us, because he knows Frank. He's a lovely guy, and he's doing brilliantly with the team.

Another coachload came into the hotel, and it was the Liverpool Academy team! They were playing the Huddersfield Academy Team, so it was a real football afternoon.

The hotel was a great place for an interview, even though the players were there to distract us!

⚽

Frank Stewart Worthington was born in Halifax, Yorkshire on 23 November, 1948.

He started his career at Huddersfield Town in 1966, and what an amazing playing career it was.

Frank has had more clubs than Tiger Woods. He has played from one side of the globe to the other. I suppose he reminds me of yours truly, because even though I didn't play at the same level as Frank, I certainly made up for it with the miles I clocked up, playing in different countries, and coaching abroad too.

❦❀

I could tell as soon as Frank walked in that he was going to be very forthcoming and open about everything. He was a ray of sunshine, and never stopped talking from the minute he sat down.

Frank stayed at Huddersfield until 1972, scoring forty-one goals in 171 appearances.

He then moved to Leicester. Frank told me that he enjoyed playing football there more than all the other clubs he played for.

While playing at Leicester, he got picked for England and made his debut against Argentina at Wembley.

Frank was really proud to play for his country.

'It's the highest accolade that any player can achieve. It just doesn't get any better than that!'

Frank's all-time favourite game was in an England shirt, playing away against Bulgaria, with Frank scoring the only goal.

When England played away games, the players would couple up and share a room together. Frank said that he always shared with ex-Sheffield United player Tony Currie.

He told me that he thought Tony Currie was a better midfield player than Glen Hoddle. He really raved on about Currie's ability.

Personally, I don't agree with Frank. Glen Hoddle was one of the best players for England in that position. Currie was a great play in his day, but not better than Glen Hoddle in my estimation.

Frank played eight games for England, and scored two goals. He really admired Sir Alf Ramsey, the England manager at the time when Frank was playing.

Frank said he was a little eccentric but that he was a great manager who studied the game throughout, in every detail.

At Leicester City, Frank scored seventy-two goals in 210 appearances.

'I really loved playing alongside Alan Birchenall,' he said. Frank told me that the ex-Chelsea player was one of the best characters he had ever met in the game and he still loves him dearly to this day. He had nothing but good to say about him. Frank remembers his time at Leicester with great fondness.

⚽

Frank left Leicester in 1977, and joined Bolton Wanderers, where he is best remembered for the "wonder goal" he scored against Ipswich Town. It really was a wonderful, one of Frank's greatest sporting achievements.

The ball was bouncing around in Ipswich's area, with Frank chasing it, with four defenders behind him, virtually in a straight line.

Frank got to the ball first and started to juggle it on each foot several times, and then in a flash, he lobbed the ball over his head, with his back to the goal, and the defenders too. He turned around and volleyed it into the corner of the net. It really was just how Frank described it: 'Sheer class.'

Frank was easy to spot on a football field. He always played with his socks rolled down, and he never wore shin guards for protection.

One thing I liked about Frank was that he was always quick to praise people from the past and didn't bear any grudges.

Frank had a strange mannerism: he kept talking about what a great scrapper he was, and how he still loved to fight, if duty called at any time.

He said he was tough because of his father's Manchester background. He taught Frank how to stand up for himself, and when we were talking, he stood up and pounded my colleague Steve Conroy in the ribs, but only in a joking way.

Steve joked afterwards that he would have to go to the casualty ward because of Frank's bullying and smashing his ribs in. We all had a laugh about it though!

It was pretty obvious that Frank was really enjoying the interview, and he remarked on how we had made him feel welcomed. Our conversation was very enlightening.

Frank scored thirty-five goals for Bolton in eighty-four appearances. In his second season with them in 1979, he was also the "top scorer" in the old Division One, with twenty-four league goals and seven others in different cup games.

He just pipped Liverpool's Kenny Dalglish to win the trophy.

Frank stayed at Bolton until 1979 and went on loan across the water to the USA, to play for Philadelphia Fury.

However, he returned to the U.K. in the same year, and joined Birmingham City, where he scored twenty-nine goals in seventy-five appearances.

In 1980, Frank then went on loan again, to Mjällby in Sweden, and on loan again the following year in 1981, to Tampa Bay Rowdies in the USA again.

Frank then joined Leeds United in 1982, scoring fourteen goals in thirty-two appearances.

Frank kept moving from club to club, enjoying his football:

Sunderland	1983	19 games	2 goals.
Southampton	1984	34 games	4 goals.
Brighton	1985	31 games	7 goals.
Tranmere	1985/87	59 games	21 goals.
Preston	1987	23 games	3 goals.

| Stockport | 1988 | 19 games | 6 goals. |
| Cape Town | 1988 | 0 games | 0 goals. |

Frank also played for numerous non-league clubs too, so you can see that I was serious when I said that he'd had more clubs than Tiger Woods.

I liked the way that Frank kept interrupting me, in a nice way, telling little stories or joking about something that had happened to him in his career.

Frank really was entertaining from beginning to end.

I asked him to name his favourite manager from all the clubs he'd been at. He just laughed and said: 'Peter Stringfellow!'

I thought that was hilarious.

After we had all stopped laughing, Frank said that his favourite manager in the football world was without a doubt, Sir Alf Ramsey.

'He was so thorough in everything he did. He studied everything that was necessary for the team. A bit of a perfectionist, but I've got the utmost respect and admiration for him,' Frank said.

I was a little shocked while listening to Frank praising Alf Ramsey so much, because Frank and Alf Ramsey are like chalk and cheese. They are total opposites. Frank is so flamboyant and wild, while Alf Ramsey is so conservative and strict. They always say that opposites attract.

I asked Frank to name the hardest defenders that he'd played against. He quickly mentioned three regular candidates:

'Norman Hunter, Ron Harris, and of course Tommy Smith. They were all dirty b*st*rds,' Frank said.

He said that once or twice when they had kicked him, he would sort them out sooner or later in the game, and when he did, they knew about it.

In contrast, Frank's best opponent was Sir Bobby Moore.

'No defender read the game like he did. He wasn't very quick on the pitch, but he was incredibly fast to assess a good or bad situation. He was the greatest defender of his time.'

Sometimes when Frank was with the England squad, Bobby Moore would take him to the infamous "Blind Beggar" pub, where Ronnie Kray murdered George Cornell and got life imprisonment for it.

The pub's landlord, Jimmy Quill, was a good friend of Bobby's. Frank liked Bobby Moore, not only as a wonderful player, but as a really nice guy.

Frank's favourite player of all time was his old mate George Best. His favourite ever player from foreign shores was Pelé. Of course, Frank is not the first ex-player in my book to mention "Georgie Boy".

When Frank was playing in the USA for the Tampa Bay Rowdies, George Best was on the other coast, playing for San

Jose Earthquakes. Every now and then, they would meet up for a drink or two.

Let's be totally honest here about how talented Frank was. He had so much skill with his close control, and he was never afraid to show it off on the pitch. He was never a particularly hard working player, but he scored some great goals in his long, illustrious career.

As skilful as Frank was, he openly admitted that George Best was the most skilful of them all. He said he could watch "Besty" every day of the week. He just loved watching him, and had a real admiration for him too. He also said that he was a lovely human being.

Frank told me that he definitely didn't have any regrets in football, apart from one. He always wanted to play for Bill Shankly at Liverpool. The chance came for Frank to sign for them, but he failed the medical because of high blood pressure.

Bill Shankly, just like Frank, also started his career at Huddersfield Town.

⚽

Frank was constantly coming out with funny "one-liners".

He said that towards the end of his playing career, he went for a check-up, and the doctor told him to get as far away as he could from football.

'So I joined Stockport County.'

I couldn't stop laughing. He made the interview so pleasant with his constant humour.

Frank still plays five-a-side football in Halifax at the ripe old age of 66, which I think is great.

Once again, out popped his tales of aggression, telling Steve and myself that if anyone on the field wanted to "mix it", then he was in like a shot, and told us that he sorted anyone out.

Frank stood up and said:

'Go on, Norm. Hit me in the stomach! Go on, lad. Just to see how hard I am!'

I was peeing myself laughing. One thing for sure is that if you ever get the chance to meet Frank Worthington, I can guarantee that you will never forget him.

A "thumbs up" from Frank Worthington.

CHAPTER FOURTEEN
KEITH HACKETT

Keith Hackett on the pitch.

My book is full of ex-players and managers, so I thought it would be refreshing to have a top referee included here, and to get his perspective on the game and his experiences.

Keith Hackett has a fine pedigree in the refereeing world. I've known him for a good few years, as a referee and also as a friend, which helped to get him on board for this book.

I've known Keith since the start of his career. He gave me a lift from one of the games I was playing and Keith was refereeing. I asked him if he was going my way, and that's how we got friendly.

I said: 'you can give me a lift as long as you don't book me!' We had a nice chat during the journey, and became friends. Of course, due to our globe-trotting careers, we've sometimes lost touch, but it was good to meet up.

When Steve and I arranged to meet Keith, it was in Chapeltown, Sheffield, in a pub called the Red Lion. It was on the main Halifax Road.

It was good to catch up with Keith, because he's now one of the top dogs in the referee world, and he's busy abroad a lot of the time.

❦❀

Keith Stuart Hackett was born in Sheffield on 22 June 1944.

He started refereeing in the local amateur leagues all around the Sheffield area and quickly made a name for himself as a referee who was "going places".

Little did Keith know at the start of his career that his refereeing would take him all around the world.

Keith got promoted quickly to the non-league (semi-professional) ranks, mainly the Northern Premier League where Keith learnt his trade and became established there for a few years.

Keith has got some great memories and stories about the Northern Premier League.

One of my favourite stories that he told me was about a game he had refereed at Boston. After the match, one of the Boston players, Jimmy Kabia, asked Keith if he could give him a ride back to Sheffield because he was stranded and he knew that Keith was from the same area as himself.

Keith answered him:

'You've got a nerve asking me for a lift, because all you did during the game was to complain about my refereeing.'

After a few other words were exchanged, Keith, being the good-hearted man that he was, gave the player a lift.

What's so ironic about this tale is that a very long time ago, I too asked Keith for a lift in the virtually the same circumstances. However, unlike Jimmy Kabia, I didn't ruffle Keith's feathers during the game or while he was driving me back.

As Keith was driving home, Kabia kept telling Keith what a bad ref he was, slandering him from pillar to post, so Keith stopped the car.

'If you don't f*cking shut up, you'll be walking back to Sheffield,' he said.

Another classic was when he was at Boston again, some time later. Boston were playing against Altringham, who had a player called Johnny King. All King wanted to do during the game was to have a dig at the referees.

Keith said that when he found himself near King, he would run in different diagonals on the pitch, so as to miss any confrontation with him. King was looking for trouble for the whole ninety minutes, and Keith thought it was wise to avoid him as it would have played havoc with his concentration.

Keith blew his whistle for the game to end, and as he was coming off the pitch, he felt an arm go across his shoulder, which finished up in another player's face, sending him to the floor.

'You're done,' Keith told King.

'Well, it was worth it,' King replied. 'Because I've been trying to f*cking get him all through the game.'

My favourite non-league story of Keith's was when he was refereeing a game at Frickley. His linesman that day was a guy called Johnny Hutton. He came to the game on his motor bike, which Keith said was very unusual. He would park his bike away from the ground, just to be on the safe side.

Keith saw Hutton ask the Frickley Chairman for £30 pounds expenses for running the line.

The Chairman said to him:

'I've seen your bike. You're not f*cking getting that much money. When you're riding that bike down steep hills, I bet you turn off the f*cking engine. Here's a fiver. Now f*ck off.'

Keith tells a great story. He's had me in stitches so many times.

⚽

At the very young age of thirty two, Keith got promoted to the football league, and he was one of their youngest ever referees at that time.

In 1980, he was in charge of the Hillsborough semi-final between Aston Villa and Liverpool. This was Keith's all-time favourite game as a referee.

Keith was then put in charge of the 1981 FA Cup Final between Tottenham Hotspur and Manchester City.

A very strange thing happened at that match. Keith had to name his preference: did he want to receive the cup final medal, or thirty five pounds for refereeing the game?

Oh well! Stranger things have happened in football.

In 1982, Keith was listed with FIFA, even though he was still only thirty-seven years old.

In 1984, he was in charge of the Charity Shield between Everton and Liverpool. Then in 1988, he refereed the European Championships, and in the same year also, the Olympic Tournament.

Unfortunately, Keith missed out on refereeing the World Cup in 1990, because of an injured Achilles tendon, which he sadly regrets, but he was very happy to have done everything else.

Keith retired from professional refereeing in 1994, at the age of fifty. I'm sure you will all agree with me that Keith Hackett put in a good shift on the refereeing circuit. Keith wasn't finished yet though.

He was appointed as the head referee throughout the football league, and later, for the Premiership.

Being a football official for all those years has had its consequences, and on two occasions it cost Keith his day-job, because he was given an ultimatum – to work or referee, and he chose to referee.

He started assessing referees, and has worked tirelessly to improve the refereeing standards throughout the football leagues and the Premiership.

He has travelled to Ethiopia, Mexico, Vietnam, the USA, and many more countries, teaching and coaching referees from the grass-roots upwards.

His knowledge is second to none in his field of expertise.

Keith has also written books about refereeing, and he even writes in the Guardian newspaper with cartoonist Paul Trevillion, in a series called 'You are the Ref'.

He has also produced a DVD for training purposes. Keith may have retired from actual refereeing, but as you can see, he's been very busy since he hung up his whistle.

Keith has been very involved with the Pro Zone technology programme, which helps football officials in every way possible. It really is a unique way of understanding and analysing football, and is an invaluable tool for referees.

Keith has kindly offered to give me a guided tour of this fascinating project, which is based in Leeds. I hope to go there in the very near future. I've heard a lot about it.

Pro Zone technology measures player statistics, and gives teams a bird's eye view of the players and their tactics.

Keith has been a consultant for quite a while now – but he makes sure that he gets some spare time, and he enjoys watching his local football team, Stocksbridge Park Steels, who play in Division One of the Northern Premier League, where Keith cut his teeth.

He has always been a Sheffield Wednesday fan, which is why his favourite game in charge as a referee was the semi-final at Hillsborough between Aston Villa and Liverpool in 1980, because when he set foot on the pitch, it brought back great memories for Keith of watching the Owls play there week after week.

He also loved refereeing the 1981 FA Cup Final between Spurs and Manchester City, because being in charge of the cup final is always going to create great memories for anyone involved.

I asked Keith what he thought about the new breed of refs working today, such as Howard Webb.

Keith told me that Webb is the best ref in the game in the UK, and that he had told Webb that he could be the best ref in the world one day. He meant every word.

He also rates Mark Clattenburg and Michael Oliver highly. Both these refs are still relatively young for the Premiership.

I had just told my colleague Steve Conroy that the present-day referee Howard Webb has very similar refereeing habits to Keith.

Little did I know that Keith had trained and coached Webb from a young age, so it turns out that my judgment about their similarities was quite accurate.

I enjoyed comparing opinions about certain rules of the game with Keith. We both agreed that the "no pass back to the keeper" rule was an excellent choice, but we also both agreed that sending off players for being the last man before a shooting chance was diabolical.

It just causes too many problems. Keith calls it the "triple jeopardy" rule.

'It's bad enough for a team having a penalty awarded against them, but to send the defender off as well just ruins the game,' he said.

Keith also thinks that refs dish out too many red cards too easily. He said when he was refereeing, a really good b*ll*cking would be enough, most of the time.

When Keith was refereeing, there were three cameras on the pitch. Now there are twenty-two. That means that the refs are on centre-stage more than ever before.

I also asked Keith what he thought about women refs, and how long it would be before we saw women refereeing in the Premiership.

He said without any hesitation that we might be seeing women referees in the Premiership in as soon as five years, which I thought was good.

He said that women refs are already active at the top levels of football in Germany and Switzerland, so it might happen here sooner than we think.

It was time for my questionnaire for Keith.

I asked him to name the favourite player that he's ever refereed.

'Kenny Dalglish,' Keith said. 'He was so professional in every game he played. His attitude never altered for the whole ninety minutes. He was a total professional, and he expected the ref to be the same. That's why he would get in the ref's face sometimes. Because he felt he should be questioned about doing his job in a professional capacity.'

Keith agreed that this was absolutely correct.

He told me one story about Dalglish. It was Big John Charles' testimonial game, between Leeds United and Juventus.

For some strange reason, Dalglish was playing for Leeds, who had a young kid playing on the wing. A pass came his way, but he just let it go by him. Immediately, Dalglish got in the young kid's face and said to him:

'You're a professional, and so you should play like a professional in every game, no matter what!'

Keith totally admires Dalglish's attitude: the way he always played at one hundred percent, from beginning to end.

The player Keith admired for other reasons was John Fashanu, most famous as a Wimbledon FC player, because of the way he spoke and explained his actions on the pitch.

Keith remembers the time Fashanu had to explain his own conduct, after a clash with Spurs player Gary Mabbutt, which resulted in Mabbutt's eye socket being broken.

Keith said that Fashanu was the most articulate and expressive footballer he had ever come across. Fashanu's command of English in explaining how the clash had come about was impeccable.

I asked Keith to name the footballer who had been the worst to referee. I was quite shocked when he mentioned Lawrie Sanchez, another Wimbledon player.

Keith said that Sanchez was always giving him problems and being belligerent.

I asked Keith to name his finest achievement in football. Keith said:

'Just helping to make referees better in every way that I can.' I thought that this statement was typical of Keith, always striving to do his best.

I also asked Keith about his fondest memories in football – and let's remember that Keith has refereed at the very top level. He's refereed at cup finals, top league games, international games, and even at the Olympics.

'Refereeing in the local leagues of Sheffield while I was learning my trade,' he said.

I thought that was a great answer to my last question.

⚽

Like I said before, I have known Keith a long time. Maybe not as a close friend, but we have always had a good word for each other, even when he was in charge of one of my games.

I do sincerely mean what I am about to say, which is that I do truly believe that Keith Hackett has played a major part in improving this country's refereeing standards throughout all the leagues and divisions, especially the finest league in the world at the moment, the Premiership.

Keith has been instrumental in bringing the likes of Howard Webb through the ranks, and many more just like him.

It's not just home-grown talent: Keith has coached many upcoming overseas referees at grass-roots level too.

Quite simply, Keith Hackett will be here for a long time yet, training and coaching our referees and improving standards in football.

He's definitely a legend of the refereeing world.

Keith Hackett and me team up for the interview.

CHAPTER FIFTEEN
SIR TOM FINNEY

I tried to arrange an interview with Tom Finney at Preston North End's Deepdale Stadium, to watch a home game together. I wanted Sir Tom to be the first interview in my book, as an iconic figure of football history.

My good friend, ex-Manchester City

Tom Finney, about to kick off for England.

player Ian Lees, was organising the meeting, but sadly, Sir Tom fell ill, and the Preston North End officials told us that Tom's illness was critical. I kept my fingers crossed for a full recovery and a future meeting.

✦☻

Like most football fans, I watch Sky Sports News to keep myself updated with all the football gossip. I will never forget 14 February 2014. I was so upset, with the headline repeating itself over and over again every few minutes, stating that the famous, well-loved footballer, Sir Tom Finney, had died, aged ninety one.

I just could not believe what I was hearing, as I was due to meet the great man very soon. Alas, now it will never happen. I was really looking forward to interviewing him.

It's so ironic – Ian and I had discussed that it would be a good idea to interview Sir Tom as soon as possible, as he was in his nineties and feeling quite frail. Unfortunately, our interview was not meant to be.

⚽

I have heard wonderful things said about Sir Tom Finney.

One story that comes to mind is the time that Preston North End played against Blackburn Rovers in a pre-season friendly. The full-back who was marking Tom was none other than Dave Whelan, now the Wigan Chairman.

It was Whelan's first match after breaking his leg in the 1960 FA Cup final. When Dave saw that he would be marking Tom, he despaired.

'It's my first match back after two and a half years, and I'm up against the finest right-winger there's ever been,' he thought. However, Whelan managed to take the ball off Tom three times in the first half, without any resistance.

'Tom, you're not taking me on,' Whelan said, puzzled, as they walked off the pitch.

'You've had some bad luck, son,' Finney replied. 'I'm not going to take you on. I want you to get through today's game and get back into the first team.'

Whelan is still full of praise and admiration for Finney's attitude towards him in that match.

How many players would have done that today?

As a true icon of the game, I decided that it was important to include Sir Tom Finney in this book.

⚽

Thomas Finney was born in Preston on the 5 April, 1922. He idolised his local team, Preston North End as he was growing up, and while he was still a teenager, his home team wanted to sign him as a professional!

Despite being rather sickly, and small and slight for his age - he was only 4 feet, 9 inches tall at the age of fourteen, he showed true talent as a striker.

However, Tom's father wouldn't let him sign for Preston North End until he had become a qualified plumber in the family firm.

Before the newly-signed teenage footballer could start playing professionally, the outbreak of World War Two delayed his career. However, Tom Finney played in wartime tournaments and for army teams in North Africa, enabling him to keep polishing his skills.

After the war, his footballing skills were in demand. At the age of twenty four, he made his first league appearance for Preston in 1946, and within a month, he made his England debut, playing against Northern Ireland, and scoring a goal to contribute to England's 7-2 victory.

Finney's plumbing skills also came in useful, as he used his second career to supplement his meagre footballing wages. He earned himself the nickname "The Preston Plumber" – with his team-mates known as "the drips"!

⚽

Unusually for most footballers, Tom Finney spent his entire career at Preston North End. He loved to play for his home team, and lived less than a stone's throw away from the ground. That is what you call real loyalty.

Unfortunately, I never got the chance to tell Sir Tom that Sir Stanley Matthews had told me what a wonderful person and great player he was. The two players had a friendly rivalry, but much mutual appreciation.

The only time Finney was tempted to leave Preston was in 1952. Prince Roberto Lanza di Trabia, the millionaire president of Palermo Football Club in Sicily, offered Tom his own villa, a sports car, and the unimaginably huge wages of £130 per month (compared to the £14 per week he received at

Preston). However, the Preston club chairman rejected the offer, and Finney remained loyal to his home team for the rest of his playing career.

Bill Shankly was Finney's team mate at Preston and he frequently praised Finney for his brilliant skills and attitude as a player.

Shankly often said that Tom Finney was the finest footballer to grace a football field. Often known as a joker, with brilliant one-liners, the former Liverpool manager was once asked whether a current star player was as good as Tom Finney. Shankly said: 'Aye, he's as good as Tommy – but then Tommy's nearly 60 now.'

⚽

Tom Finney scored thirty times for England, and made seventy six appearances for his national team.

Finney played numerous times for England on the right-wing. He played numerous times on the left-wing, and also a few times in the centre-forward position.

He was so versatile, full of trickery, and he had a great body swerve. He was also a talented crosser of the ball.

In his whole playing career, Tom Finney was never booked or sent off. He was a complete gentleman on and off the field.

Unfortunately, despite such a great career, the only trophy he ever won with his dear old Preston was the Second Division

Championship in 1950-51. Preston North End appeared in the FA Cup Final in 1954, but Preston lost 3-2 to West Bromwich Albion. Finney regretted not being fully fit in that final.

Tom Finney won "The Footballer of the Year "award in 1954 and again in 1957.

He reluctantly retired, aged thirty eight, in 1960, due to a persistent groin injury, and concentrated on building up his successful plumbing business. He also worked as a reporter for the News of the World, and served as a magistrate in Preston and as the chairman of the local health authority.

Tom became the Life President of Preston North End, and a statue by Peter Hodgkingson, showing him in action on a waterlogged pitch in 1956, was unveiled in 2004.

Tom Finney was awarded the OBE in 1961, and then the CBE in 1992, and he was knighted in 1998, which was not a surprise for many people, as most people in the media and the football world thought that this honour was long overdue and 100% deserved.

Tom Finney will be sadly missed, not only as a football hero, but as a wonderful, kind and humble human being throughout his life.

I just regret that I did not get to meet him in time.

Sir Tom Finney as an elder statesman of football.

CHAPTER SIXTEEN
DAVID LAYNE

David Layne: "Bronco", in his Sheffield Wednesday prime.

A mutual friend helped me to get hold of David Layne, and we met in a pub in Sheffield called the White Rose. The pub was busy, with a teatime carvery crowd, and David brought his wife with him.

David was my boyhood hero, and it was great to talk to him about his football career, and although he wasn't as forthcoming or chatty as some of my interviewees, he still had a lot to say about the state of football today.

⚽

David Layne was born in Sheffield on 29 July 1939.

He started off playing for Rotherham United in 1957, but within a year, he moved on, to Swindon Town.

At Swindon, Layne became an instant hit with the fans, scoring twenty-eight goals in just forty-one games.

Layne's playing attracted Bradford City and by the very next season, he was back in Yorkshire as a Bradford City player, banging in the goals again, breaking Bradford's scoring record, and netting thirty-four goals in a single season.

Most people remember David Layne by his nickname, "Bronco", which was from a television series in the sixties. Actor Ty Hardin played the main character, Bronco Layne, and the name stuck with David through the years. However, I can tell you from personal experience that David hates to be called Bronco!

As David earned his reputation as a prolific goal-scoring machine, bigger clubs were starting to take notice, and in 1962, another Yorkshire club came in for him: my much-loved Sheffield Wednesday. The Owls paid £22,500 for David Layne, which was a record fee for any Bradford player at that time.

⚽

David had a very good career with all the clubs he played with, but he will always be remembered for his great goal-scoring feats for Sheffield Wednesday.

When the Owls were in the top division, he scored fifty-two goals in only seventy-four appearances, and in one season, he scored thirty goals, which still is a record today in the top flight.

David's record has stood for over fifty years, which is quite an achievement.

It was also about this time that people started speculating about David stepping up a notch, and saying that maybe an England call-up was not very far away.

Most football pundits would probably tell you that David was ready, and was definitely good enough to play for the national team, but a severe problem stopped David in his tracks.

€☺

In 1964, David Layne, Tony Kaye, and Peter Swan were found guilty of match fixing in a betting scandal.

They were all Sheffield Wednesday players. They were each sentenced to prison for six months each. Most people thought that this punishment was very harsh, considering that the scandal was all blown out of proportion. Each player received a life ban from any participation in football.

The ban was lifted eight years later, and David re-joined Sheffield Wednesday in 1972. However, he couldn't secure a regular place in the first team, and so he went on loan to Hereford United. He retired from league football in 1973, having played only four games at the club.

David Layne then joined Matlock Town Football Club, until he finally retired through injury.

I asked David what he thought about the game of today, and he thought that the way teams play now doesn't create as many chances for goals as there were back in his day.

I'm not sure if I agree with that statement, because the playing systems are totally different compared with David's footballing prime in the early sixties, when a 2-3-5 system was the standard, compared to the modern 4-3-3 or 4-4-2, for example.

We still see lots of goals every week, so I guess that is just David's own opinion about the game as he sees it, and for sure he would know, being an ex–striker, and may I say, a very good one at that.

David's favourite goal was the one he scored in 1962, against the mighty Brazilian team Santos. Their line-up included the great player Pelé:

'We lost 2-4, but it was a great game to play in.'

I asked David to name his hardest opponent. He just said: 'None of them. They were all the same, and if they kicked me, I kicked them back.'

David's all-time favourite player is the master of the dribble, Stanley Matthews.

Nowadays, David is a retired pub landlord, and he doesn't have much to do with football.

I first met David in the late nineties when I was on holiday in Thailand, travelling with a group of friends.

Somehow, David and I ended up sharing the same hotel room for three weeks, because we were the last two to book onto the holiday.

He was quite sporty then, and I have fond memories of us playing table tennis and tennis together. David was also a good golfer, and we enjoyed some games, although my golfing really isn't as good as his!

Although now well into his seventies, David still plays golf every week, and enjoys getting onto the greens.

David was a great striker, and it's a shame that he missed out on his chance to play for England. I think all great strikers should be remembered, and I, for one, will always remember David "Bronco" Layne.

In the carvery with David Layne.

186

CHAPTER SEVENTEEN
KENNY BURNS

Kenny Burns in his 1970s
Notts Forest strip

I contacted Kenny through the PFA, the Football Players' Association. I'd sent them a letter for each of ex-players I wanted to contact.

Kenny kindly phoned me up a few weeks later. It was a sad occasion for him, though, as he'd lost his brother the day before, and he was due to travel up to his hometown in Scotland for the funeral.

Nottingham Forest was the scene of his greatest sporting triumphs. Kenny is still living in the Nottingham / Derby area and is still very fond of that part of the country.

At first, I thought that Kenny's choice of meeting place was strange, the Derby Garden Centre.

In actual fact, it was a wonderful place for an interview. I've never been to such a big garden centre in my life! We had a good walk around first, and then settled down in a secluded corner of the restaurant for our interview. I can thoroughly recommend it – for meetings and interviews, as well as gardening supplies!

❦☻

Kenny Burns was born in Glasgow on 23 September, 1953.

He started his football career with his beloved Rangers when he was just seventeen years old. Kenny loved playing for the club which he had followed throughout his childhood in Glasgow.

Kenny had always idolized Rangers ever since he was a boy. Rebelliously, the first time Rangers approached Kenny, he turned them down, and his brothers refused to talk to him. Kenny waited until the second time that Rangers came knocking before signing as an apprentice professional, and so all was well again in the Burns household.

He didn't think he would have much chance of playing in the Rangers' first team at that time, and so he decided to try elsewhere, and Kenny moved south of the border to sign for English club Birmingham City.

❦☻

It didn't take long for Kenny Burns to settle in Birmingham, and he was soon a regular player in the centre-half position, and also as a centre-forward.

Team-mate Howard Kendall had a big impression on the young Scotsman, and Kenny loved playing alongside him:

'Howard was a born leader in every sense of the word. He was a real inspiration.'

Kenny quickly made a name for himself at the midlands team, despite still being in his teens.

Kenny Burns told us about his time at Birmingham City, and had Steve and I crying with laughter. Some of the stories he told us are unrepeatable, but this one just shows Kenny's naughty side, and it's straight from the "horse's mouth".

One day, Kenny was playing away for Birmingham at Anfield against Liverpool. The opposing team's "hard man", Tommy Smith, got into Kenny's face.

Kenny spat at him and in the heat of the moment, told him to: 'F*ck off, you ugly c*nt!'

After the game, Smith came looking for Kenny in Birmingham City's dressing room but couldn't find him.

The Birmingham City players had hidden Kenny in the boot skip to keep him safe from Tommy Smith on the rampage, and they didn't let him out until they had got on the motorway.

To be fair to Kenny, he told me that this was the lowest point of his career, but he was only seventeen at the time, and I remember how bad I was at that age too! The way that Kenny told the story was so funny that he should have been a comedian, not a footballer.

※

Kenny started his career as a defender, but he was converted to a striker in 1974 when Birmingham City sold Bob Latchford to Everton.

Burns' performance as a striker for Birmingham City was impressive. He scored forty five goals in 170 games in his six years playing for the club, including three hat-tricks.

He scored three goals past his old mate Peter Shilton in a game against Leicester City in 1976. One of those goals is Kenny's all-time favourite, but he can't choose which one!

The young Scottish footballer was proving himself, but things were about to change dramatically for young Kenny.

※

Peter Taylor, Brian Clough's partner at Nottingham Forest, spotted Kenny while he was enjoying a flutter at the local dog track. Soon enough, Kenny Burns joined Brian Clough's Notts Forest for £150,000, in 1977.

When Kenny joined Forest, little did he know what a roller-coaster ride of success he was about to enjoy.

"Cloughie" converted Kenny to playing centre-back again, resulting in outstanding performances. Kenny was voted the PWA Player of the Year in the 1977/78 season, which was a great accolade for a footballer in a new team, playing in a new position.

Kenny had some great stories to share with me about his time at Forest. He said that one particular time, Clough had fined him fifty quid for a bad pass.

'The following Saturday, Notts Forest were playing Aston Villa, and Peter Withe took the kick-off and passed to Tony Woodcock, who passed to John McGovern, who then passed to me. Right away, I passed it to Larry Lloyd, saying to him: 'Hey Larry! You have the f*cking ball – I can't afford another f*cking fifty quid!"

Cloughie fined Kenny fifty quid once again when Kenny was playing against Arsenal. They had a free kick, and Kenny head-butted Arsenal's Richie Powling.

The referee didn't see the incident, but it was shown on TV, and Brian Clough was quick to penalise Kenny for his actions.

Later, Kenny was asked why he had head-butted Powling. He simply replied: 'Well, I just didn't want to be in the wall and spoil my good looks.'

Kenny joked with me about making a career on his dashing good looks. He was constantly taking the p*ss out of himself. Kenny was a breath of fresh air. I really liked the way that he didn't take himself seriously at all. He just told it how it is.

Brian Clough (with the help of Peter Taylor), had moulded the Notts Forest team bit by bit, or should I say, player by player.

It was a strategy that paid off.

Nottingham Forest were crowned Division One Champions in the 1977/78 season. In the same season, the team won the Football League Cup and the FA Charity Shield.

In 1978/9, Forest won the Football League Cup again and they also won the much coveted European Cup, and unbelievably, the European Super Cup.

Kenny and his team-mates' trophy cabinet was not full yet. In 1979/80, against all odds, they won the European Cup for a second time as back-to-back winners.

Not bad for a little club from Nottingham. It was a great feat indeed.

Kenny told me that Forest never practised free kicks or corners. I couldn't believe it!

Cloughie would just say: 'If it's a direct free kick, just f*cking shoot. If it's an indirect free kick, then pass it and then f*cking shoot.'

I found it amazing that such a great team never practised any "set pieces" at all. You have to admit that it's hard to swallow, but Kenny assured me that this is 100% true.

Kenny said that the late seventies were great years at Forest, not only for the amount of trophies they won but the camaraderie with the players.

To win the European Cup once was great, but to win it a second time consecutively was really outstanding.

Kenny explained that other managers would single out certain players from the opposition before the game and advise their team on how they would play and what they would do.

Not Cloughie or Pete Taylor. Before each game, they would just say to each player:

'You – number six! You – number five!' and so on.

No matter how unorthodox Clough and Tayler were, you have to give them credit for their achievements at Forest. They were phenomenal to say the least.

Kenny told me that Cloughie was strict, but always fair:

'He would dish out lots of b*ll*ckings, but then he would also give praise when it was deserved.'

When I asked Kenny to name the favourite manager he'd played under, he had no hesitation in naming Brian Clough, of course.

Kenny's favourite team that he'd played for would be Forest too, but he said that he loved playing for Birmingham just as much, even though he never won any silverware with them. He couldn't choose between them at all.

He has fond memories of playing in the Bernabéu stadium against Real Madrid. Kenny loved the atmosphere there, which is something that he will never forget.

When Forest got into the European Cup in 1978/9, Kenny had to go and get his passport renewed. He thought that he would be travelling to some exotic places. However, when the draw for the first round was made, Forest got Liverpool.

Kenny was so p*ssed off. He said he'd rushed about getting his passport, but he didn't even need it.

The first game was played at the Forest ground. The Liverpool captain, Emlyn Hughes, kept running around the pitch after Forest had scored their first goal, chanting: 'One goal's not enough to take you to Anfield.'

Then Forest scored their second goal. Kenny went up to Hughes and asked: 'Emlyn, is two goals enough to take us to Anfield?'

It was enough. It was the start of a run that took Forest all the way to victory in the European cup, so Kenny's reply to Hughes was very appropriate, as well as funny.

Kenny said that there would be no problem for Forest at Anfield or anywhere else, because the team knew how to keep a clean sheet. Kenny remarked that other teams couldn't score three goals against them, because Forest knew how to defend a lead.

Kenny told us another classic tale, about his all-time favourite game, the final of the European Cup against

Hamburg. The teams were about to walk out of the tunnel, and Larry Lloyd was standing next to his old mate Kevin Keegan (then playing for Hamburg), with Kenny standing nearby. Lloyd said to Keegan: 'Burnsie is having you tonight'.

Kenny was chewing some red gum, and Lloyd said to Keegan: 'Look, Burnsie's chewing meat already.'

Kenny replied: 'I'll give Keegan his fair do's.'

In the match, Kenny kept his promise. 'We had a fifty-fifty challenge on the half-way line, with both of us going in hard, and I caught him, but we both got up and just got on with the game. There was nothing said between us and no badness at all.'

Kenny's fondest Forest memories were of games playing against Europe's top teams like Juventus, AC Milan, Inter Milan, Real Madrid and Benfica. He loves looking back on the teams, the games, the fans, and the stadiums.

In four seasons at Forest, Kenny played 137 games and scored thirteen goals.

However, like everything in life, it had to end sometime.

⚽

Kenny Burns moved to Leeds United in 1981, for a fee of £400,000. He played fifty-six games, scoring just two goals.

He stayed at Leeds for three years and then in 1984, moved to Derby County.

Kenny said it was okay at Leeds but nothing special compared to what he had experienced at Forest or Birmingham.

He only stayed a year at Derby, appearing in thirty-eight games and scoring two goals, and then in 1985, he moved again for the last time in the football league, to Barnsley. He played in twenty-one games, without scoring.

Kenny then played at numerous non-league clubs, before retiring in 1993 at the age of thirty-nine, having had an illustrious career by any standards.

He told me that during his entire career, he was only sent off once, which was when he played for Leeds.

That made me laugh. I couldn't believe that he'd only been red-carded once in his career, because he was known as a "hard man" of the game.

Kenny also played internationally for Scotland. He played twenty times for his national team and scored just the one goal. He was chosen for the 1978 World Cup squad under manager Ally MacLeod, but Scotland lost the first game to Peru, and drew 1-1 in the second game with Iran.

In the final game against the Netherlands, Scotland won 3-2, with Archie Gemmill scoring his famous goal.

However, Kenny Burns had been dropped from the team for the final group match, and Scotland failed to make it to the second round. Kenny was left feeling sore. He vowed to make himself better at keeping a clean sheet and not let any goals get through, and sure enough, Forest's European Cup success was set to follow.

We didn't talk much about his international career. I just thought it was probably nothing to shout about compared to his club achievements, so we moved onto other topics.

Kenny kept entertaining Steve and myself with classic one-liners.

When Cloughie had just signed Larry Lloyd at Forest, Lloyd said to Cloughie:

'Well, boss, how do you want me to play today?'

Clough replied: 'If you don't know how to play, son, then I wasted my money buying you.'

Kenny commented that he'd seen Lloyd a while ago and his weight had shot up to twenty-six stone, which is almost double what it was when he was playing. However, Lloyd has now turned himself around and is now in great shape again – something he had to do sooner or later.

Kenny told me that his hardest opponent was John Richards of Wolverhampton Wanderers. He said he was very quick and tricky, and that his striking partner, Andy Gray, was a handful too.

He initially named Denis Law as his all-time favourite player, but then unveiled his true favourite, Rangers legend

Jim Baxter. His nickname was "Slim Jim", but after he finished playing, he became a publican and gained so much weight, he ended up at well over twenty stones. I also remember him as a great player, but unfortunately, he is no longer with us.

Ken took a self-deprecating look at himself after he had mentioned his favourite players and ex-team-mates.

'Well Norm, how much do you think they would pay for me today?' he laughed, while rubbing his belly. 'Not f*cking much for this fat b*st*rd.'

I asked Kenny Burns what he considers to be his greatest achievement.

'Just being able to play football and enjoying all the accolades I got from it,' he said. I thought that was a great answer, and he was very sincere about it.

Kenny talked about some of the great players that he'd had had the pleasure to play with or against, such as John Robertson, Eddie Gray and Kenny Dalglish, and he sang very high praises for mid-fielder Tony Currie, rating him as good as anyone else in his day.

He thinks the players from a few decades ago were much more talented than those of today. They didn't go falling and screaming every time they were tackled. Kenny says that he hates the cheats and divers in the game now: 'it's ruining our lovely game.'

Kenny can't understand why we are changing our game in the Premiership.

'Back in the eighties, we had Nottingham Forest, Aston Villa and Liverpool, all winning the European Cup, so why the need to change? If it's not broken, don't fix it.'

He loves Real Madrid's Ronaldo, but Kenny doesn't think he would score as many goals in England because he feels the quality in Spain is no longer there, and the same goes for Messi.

However, he does love to watch Southampton, because they break with pace all the time and they have so many quick players, who just love to run at defenders.

⚽

Kenny made humour from everything as we talked, and he really was such a pleasure to interview.

I can see why the Forest fans still love him at the City ground.

Until a few years ago, Kenny was working for Forest, writing articles and running hospitality, but for some reason, Forest manager Billy Davies had issues about some of Kenny's reporting and decided to terminate his contract a few years ago. However, Kenny Burns still writes a football column for the Nottingham Post.

I did ask Kenny what he would like to be doing now. He said that he would probably make a decent coach. He truly believes that he could make a difference to each player.

I can well believe that, after seeing Kenny play so many times. I think he'd make a great coach, despite not having any coaching badges or certificates of any kind. Kenny joked that the only badge he processes is from the Boys Brigade.

Well, no matter what Kenny does in the future, I'm sure he will be a success. He's so likeable, and that's a great quality.

I hope our paths cross again, because Kenny is the kind of guy who lights up a room without making any noise. He just has great charisma.

It was a real pleasure to talk to Kenny Burns: a true character on the field, and off it.

Kenny Burns keeping me enthralled in the garden centre.

CHAPTER EIGHTEEN
JIMMY GREAVES

Jimmy Greaves is the only ex-player on my list whom I didn't meet, didn't interview on the phone, and is still alive (and going strong).

Jimmy was my all-time goal-scoring hero, for Tottenham Hotspur, when I was a kid. I've always loved Jimmy Greaves,

Jimmy Greaves in his Tottenham Hotspur prime.

and I still think he's the best ever English goal-scorer.

I wrote to him, but I didn't get a reply, and I'm not sure he got the letter. However, I felt that I couldn't leave him out of my book.

⚽

James Peter Greaves was born in East Ham, London on the 20 February, 1940.

He started his career at Chelsea in 1956, and quickly rose through the ranks to make his first team debut at the age of 17.

While at Chelsea, he became the youngest ever player to reach a century of goals, and believe it or not, that record still stands today.

He scored a total of 124 goals in just 157 appearances, which is incredible by any standards, I'm sure you will agree.

He married his wife Irene in 1958, and life seemed wonderful for the talented young footballer.

⚽

Tragedy hit Jimmy Greaves in 1961, when his first child, Jimmy Jnr, died of pneumonia at the age of just four months. His death has haunted Greaves and his wife Irene for their whole lives.

Meanwhile, Greaves' goal-scoring prowess had gained the attention of Italian team A. C. Milan, who offered him a lot of money to transfer.

Jimmy was uncertain about making the move, but Milan's offer was lucrative. A move to Italy for Jimmy and Irene seemed like a good way to escape the heartache about the death of their child.

In the end, Greaves only lasted in Milan for six months. He just could not settle there. The training regime was strict, with little personal freedom for the players, not leaving much time for a home life.

He was also homesick for London. This culture shock does happen sometimes to players who move to different countries to play.

I remember when I was playing in Australia for Pan-Hellenic. A player joined us from Birmingham called Billy

Walls. He was only with us for about three weeks or so before he decided to go back to England, and he broke his two year contact with the club. The Sydney heat was just too much for him. I think he arrived in January, which was very cold in England at that time back in 1973, but it was the height of the Australian Summer, so you don't have to be a detective to work out why he couldn't stand the sudden change in temperature, let alone playing in it.

Jimmy did manage to play a dozen games in Milan and scored nine goals, which is a very good scoring ratio in Italian football because of their so-called defensive attitude towards the game.

⚽

Greaves returned to his native England, and in the same year, Tottenham Hotspur signed him for £99,999.

There was a good reason for the unusual transfer fee, as "Spurs" manager Bill Nicholson didn't want to embarrass Jimmy by making him the first £100,000 player in British football.

It didn't take long for Jimmy to get back into his goal-scoring routine and he revelled in his time at White Hart Lane, back in his comfort zone in London.

Jimmy had nine great years at "Spurs", and broke the club record by scoring 220 goals in 321 appearances.

His goal scoring record at Hotspur is second to none, and he also finished as the Top Scorer in Division One for four years as a Tottenham player, a phenomenal record.

❦

In 1970, Greaves moved on to West Ham for £54,000.

In his debut match, he scored two goals for the "Hammers", contributing to a 5-1 win against Manchester City.

However, he only stayed at West Ham for one season, scoring thirteen goals in thirty-eight appearances.

Struggling with his fitness and his motivation, Greaves was sliding into bad habits. He started drinking more and more alcohol, often going to the pub straight after training sessions, and one late-night drinking bout with team-mates in January 1971, led to a 4-0 FA Cup defeat to Blackpool.

Greaves left West Ham following his last appearance in May 1971, a 1-0 defeat against Huddersfield Town.

❦

Throughout the 70s, Greaves had a bad drinking problem, at times, drinking twenty pints of lager during the day and a bottle of vodka in the evening. For two years after leaving West Ham, he had nothing to do with football, eventually returning to the game to play for various Non-League teams before finally retiring from playing.

He'd hit hard times in the seventies, with bankruptcy, time spent in a mental hospital, and his wife Irene divorcing him.

He stopped drinking suddenly in February 1978. He decided to walk away from alcohol, and hasn't touched a drop since, becoming completely teetotal.

⚽

Jimmy Greaves managed to piece his life back together. Reunited with his wife and family, he started writing a regular football column for the Sun newspaper, and appeared as a TV football pundit.

Greaves' witty one-liners led to a lucky break in 1985, when he joined forces with another ex-footballer, Ian St. John to co-host hosted the light-hearted ITV football show *Saint and Greavsie*. It was an instant success, mainly because of Greavsie's dry humour, with Ian St John as the "straight man".

The show flourished for seven years before it came to an end in 1992 in the advent of Sky Sports winning the rights to the newly-formed Premier League from ITV.

⚽

Jimmy Greaves does the odd "after dinner" speech and he is still occasionally seen on TV.

He's certainly a character that football will never forget, mainly because of his great goal-scoring feats, domestically, and internationally too.

He scored a total of 366 goals in 528 appearances in the football league. Is there anyone with a better record?

He also scored forty-four goals in only fifty-seven appearances for England. He played in the 1966 World Cup squad, playing in all the group games against Uruguay, Mexico and France.

Disaster struck in the match against France when he was injured, requiring fourteen stitches to his shin, and had to endure the momentous final from the back of the grandstand, unable to share in his team-mates' glory. Who knows how differently things could have turned out?

Even though circumstances meant that he missed his biggest chance to shine, I will always say that Jimmy Greaves is the best striker England ever had, and I do mean ever.

I was quite upset that I couldn't get hold of Jimmy for an interview for this book because I knew that he would be a ray of sunshine. I cannot remember once seeing him on TV without wearing a smile. Jimmy has that certain charisma that only some people have, and I just know that if I was in the same room as "Greavsie", we would have had a ball while talking about his life and past experiences.

Sadly, I couldn't ask him all the usual questions such as: "Who is his favourite all-time player?", and "What's your favourite ever goal?" I like to think that his favourite player is me! (Ha-ha!)

Jimmy Greaves will always be one of the all-time greats in my book.

Jimmy Greaves with his trademark 'tache.

CHAPTER NINETEEN
PETER LORIMER

Peter Lorimer in 1968.

I arranged to meet Peter through his former Leeds United teammate Eddie Gray.

These days, Peter is a pub landlord. He runs the Commercial Inn in Holbeck, Leeds, where we chatted to Eddie.

The inner city Holbeck area of Leeds is quite run down, and I was a bit surprised that Peter hadn't opted for a more upmarket establishment, but his pub is within walking distance of the Leeds ground and is a haven for football fans.

Peter is still also earning a wage through football, doing radio work and ambassador work for his old club.

🦶⚽

Peter Patrick Lorimer was born in Dundee, Scotland on 14 December, 1946.

Peter had a good school-boy football career and played for Scotland boys, and in one game against England, he scored four goals.

He caught the eye of local talent scouts, but he decided to move south. Manchester United were very interested in signing Peter, but he opted for Leeds United, at the time managed by the infamous Don Revie, for his chance of making the grade. The rest is history.

Peter made his debut in the first team for Leeds at the age of fifteen, an incredibly young age. This tells you how highly-rated he was by the team's manager.

After Lorimer's debut, Revie left him out of the team for a couple of years so he could mature. The tactic paid off. In the 1966 season, Lorimer scored nineteen goals, more than any other Leeds player that season.

Peter had a great career at Leeds, spanning an incredible seventeen years. He was widely known as "Thunderboots", because of his tremendous shooting power. The only other player I can remember with shooting power like Peter was Ipswich Town's Ted Philips.

He was a prolific goal-scorer from season to season, and became Leeds United's all-time top goal-scorer, totalling 238 goals in 703 appearances. I thought he must be the team's most prolific player.

However, Peter amazed me when he said that Norman Hunter, Jack Charlton, Billy Bremner and Paul Madeley had also appeared more than 700 times for Leeds United, and that Paul Reaney, Johnny Giles, and Eddie Gray were not far behind too.

⚽

Peter's favourite goal was in the semi-final of the European Cup, playing against Barcelona:

'Scoring in that atmosphere in Barcelona's own back yard was incredible,' Peter said. 'That memory will stay in my heart forever.'

His favourite game was the Centennial Cup Final against Arsenal. 'Let's face it, Norm. It has to be the most memorable game, because the Queen was there watching, and she's not going to be there for the next Centennial Cup Final, is she?'

Unusually, after winning that Cup Final, the FA made Leeds play their next league game against Wolves just two days afterwards, on a Monday evening. That would never happen now. Peter assured me that this actually happened, although I find it hard to believe.

Peter thinks that playing at Wembley is devalued nowadays, as football league play-offs and FA Cup semi-finals are held at the stadium too.

'In my day, it was a real honour to play there. It really meant something.'

Peter totally agreed with his ex-team-mate, Eddie Gray, when I asked him about his hardest opponents.

Remember, Peter was a winger, just like Eddie. He wasn't as orthodox as Eddie in the general sense, but he came face-to-face with people like Tommy Smith, Eddie McCredie, Ron Harris, and of course Peter Storey.

Peter thought that Peter Storey was the worst of the lot for kicking and violence. 'He was a real animal. I knew what to expect every time I played against him. I was no pussy-cat, though. I could take care of myself when I needed to.'

We also talked about the high wages that players now get, like Yaya Touré of Manchester City, who earns wages of around £250,000 per week. These figures seem unbelievable, when you think that Peter and his fellow players didn't earn that much in their entire careers.

However, Peter is not jealous or envious. 'Good luck to them. It's not their fault. It's Sky TV that's made all this happen. If the players can get it, then good luck to them!'

We also discussed what's happening with the development and improvement of young British players.

'Steve Gerrard was the last decent British player to come through Liverpool's academy in seventeen years,' Peter said. I could hardly believe it, but that's that the sad truth. Very little British talent actually comes through those expensive academies.

It does make you wonder what and how the kids are coached there. Peter also thinks that it is harder for a British kid to make the grade, because of all the foreign talent coming from overseas.

Eddie Gray was 100% correct when he said that all the best players come from the slum areas of the world.

In contrast, in the UK, when parents take their kids to the academies, they really think that after five, six or seven years, they are definitely going to be signed by their clubs.

'But a lot of them are there just to make the numbers up,' Peter said.

⚽

Leeds United won a lot of trophies while Peter was in the team:

Football League Division One Winners 1968/69,
Runners-up 1965/66, 1969/70, 1970/71, 1971/72.
FA Cup Winners 1972, Runners-up 1970, and 1973.
Football League Cup Winners 1968.

Inter-Cities Fairs Cup Winners 1968 and 1971,
Runners-up 1967.

European Cup Winners Cup 1973.

European Cup Runners-up 1975.

As you can see, Peter's tally is quite impressive to say the least.

⚽

Just like Eddie Gray, Peter didn't have a long playing career with Scotland. He only played twenty-one games for his national team, scoring just four goals.

'Scotland didn't really play a lot of international games, compare with other countries like England. And Mr Revie didn't like to let us go, in case we missed a vital Leeds match, or we got injured.'

Revie's tactic of using the same players over and over again had its drawbacks. Peter told me that there were lots of other good players in the Leeds team, who weren't utilised to their full potential, such as Terry Hibberd, Rod Belfitt, Mick Bates and Jimmy Greenhoff. For some reason, Revie would never play them unless he had to.

He loved to keep the same team as often as possible, and of course, that had its price. When Leeds played Celtic in the semi-final of the European Cup, only a few days before they had played Manchester United in another semi, the Leeds players were just knackered.

Peter told me that when Leeds lost in the European Cup Final against Bayern Munich in Paris 1975, he felt very sad.

Not just because his goal was disallowed, but because Don Revie had left Leeds United to become the new England Manager.

Peter and the rest of the players had wanted to win the game for Don – because it was really Don Revie's team that had got them to the final, even though Jimmy Armfield was now managing Leeds.

It was the beginning of the end of the so-called "Leeds machine".

A lot of the big names were at the end of their careers and new blood needed injecting in the team. Some say that's the reason why Revie left the team for the England post – but then what manager wouldn't jump at the chance to manage England?

Peter left Leeds in 1979, and went to play across the water for Toronto Blizzard, playing thirty-one games and scoring nine goals in the season.

Then he returned to the UK and played for York City, before returning to Toronto for the 1980 season, playing in eighteen games and scoring just two goals.

In 1981-83, he played on the West Coast of Canada, for the Vancouver Whitecaps, playing eighty-seven games and scoring twenty-three goals.

He then returned to England, and in 1984, he played once again for Leeds United, making seventy-six appearances and scoring seventeen goals, to end a wonderful career in the football league.

⚽

Peter is still working at Leeds United. He commentates on match days, and he is also a club ambassador, along with his old playing pal Eddie Gray.

He watches every Leeds game, home and away.

Running the Commercial Inn also keeps him near to the Elland Road ground. He's been there over twenty years, and he has lots of other interests to keep himself busy.

If Peter has a legacy in the game, then it must be for his tremendously hard shooting ability, which will be remembered for a long, long time.

Norm and Peter Lorimer at the Commercial.

CHAPTER TWENTY
MALCOLM MACDONALD

"Supermac" in action!

I wrote to Newcastle United in the hope of interviewing Malcolm Macdonald, and I was delighted when he emailed me back with his phone number.

I called him up and he said that if it was convenient, we should meet up at the pub near his house.

These days, Malcolm lives in a little place outside Whitley Bay, called Seaton Sluice. It's a picturesque fishing village, on the mouth of the Seaton Burn River.

Malcolm's got a house on the riverside, and it's just a short walk to the pub where we met. Malcolm had just had knee surgery, and he needed gentle exercise. We had a good look around the historic village, followed by a great interview.

Neither Steve or I ever heard of the village before, but we both thought it was very beautiful, with its harbour, and a great view out to sea.

We held our interview in the back conservatory of the pub, where we had a good view of the harbour.

Malcolm Ian Macdonald was born in Fulham, London on 7 January, 1950.

He started his playing days at Tonbridge Angels in Kent as a full-back, and he even played right and left sides too, but he mainly played left, because the manager, Harry Haslam then had a left footed left-back. Malcolm told me that Haslam didn't want to upset the other player, so he played Malcolm on the right. He also played Macdonald up-front a few times, with very good results.

The young amateur player was soon noticed by his local professional club, Fulham. In 1968, Macdonald signed as a professional player, for a fee of only £1,000.

The manager of the club was the well-known Bobby Robson, and Malcolm was actually his very first signing. Malcolm's old manager from Tonbridge, Harry Haslam, was also now at Fulham.

Haslam kept telling Robson to play Macdonald upfront, because of his speed, and he also assured Robson that Malcolm would score goals for him in that position

However, Macdonald only spent one year at Fulham.

'I was very unhappy with things there,' Malcolm said.

At the time, Fulham had the first football league player to earn £100 a week: Johnnie Haynes. He was worshiped at the "Craven Cottage".

Malcolm laughed as he told me that before Haynes' wages went up to £100 a week, he used to drive an old Ford Popular car, but as soon as he got his big pay rise, Haynes bought a nice new Jaguar. Just three days after he bought it, Haynes crashed the car right outside the ground.

Bobby Robson tried to change things at Fulham by trying to get the old players out and get some youth into the team, but the Fulham board, and Chairman Tommy Trinder (the music hall comedian) were having none of it.

Malcolm wanted to leave the stifling atmosphere at Fulham, and said to Tommy Trinder: 'If you don't let me go, then I will get Johnnie Haynes in a corner and I shall beat the living daylights out of him.'

Malcolm said that players like Johnnie Haynes were like gods to the fans and no way would they be getting rid of players like him. The club's devotion to its "old guard" disillusioned the young Macdonald.

⚽

In 1969, Malcolm Macdonald got his wish and moved to Luton Town. He played centre-forward, scoring a very creditable goal tally of almost fifty goals in less than ninety games. Macdonald was the top scorer for two seasons running, and soon, other clubs were noticing this young, quick striker with an eye for goals.

There's a rumour that's been floating around the grapevine, suggesting that Malcolm actually played full-back for most of his time in Luton.

Malcolm assured me that this was no more than just speculation, although he did play in that position for a few odd times in certain emergencies.

Macdonald had a great respect for the Luton manager, Alex Stock, even if he sometimes had a very eccentric way of doing things.

At the beginning of the season, Stock would walk into the dressing room and explain to each player, from number 1 to 11, what he wanted from them.

The manager would go down the line of players, telling each of them how many goals he should score in the season to come. When he reached Malcolm, he said that he would be expecting 30 goals!

'Stock was the only manager I ever heard talking about promotion chances before the season had even started,' Malcolm said. 'But some of my friends said he'd done the same at other clubs.'

No one laughed behind Alex Stock's back at his unusual methods, because he was well-liked as a manager. 'I had two great years at Luton under Alex Stock, and he was a pleasure to work under.'

As a top goal-scorer, Malcolm was now getting lots of publicity.

Newcastle United had been watching his progress closely, and in 1971, Newcastle's manager Joe Harvey, paid £180,000 for Macdonald's services.

❦

Malcolm had a wonderful "Magpies" debut against Liverpool, scoring a hat-trick.

He continued scoring for them for five seasons, swiftly becoming Newcastle United's top scorer and earning his famous nickname, "Supermac".

The Newcastle fans loved him for what he was, a goal-scoring machine, hitting ninety-five goals in just 187 appearances.

Malcolm told me a great story about Bill Shankly, the Liverpool manager at that time. When Newcastle played at Anfield, they had to pass through a very low tunnel, with steps from the dressing room to the pitch.

Attached to the wall on these steps was a large red sign with the Liverpool Football Club logo, which read "This is Anfield".

Malcolm said that Shankly had deliberately lowered the ceiling, so that all the away teams had to "bow" to Liverpool

Football Club. The sign, and the low ceiling, are still there to this day, an essential part of Liverpool FC mythology.

When Malcolm met the Liverpool boss for the first time, he asked: 'So this is Anfield?"

Shankly quickly replied: 'Aye, lad, it is. And you will soon know that you're in the right place for sure, laddy. You can run but you can't hide.'

Malcolm could surely run, and score goals, without hiding.

He really enjoyed his stay at Newcastle, and I could hardly believe it when he told me that the first team squad had only thirteen players in total, for the whole season. He also told me that the greatest Liverpool team of the 80s also only had thirteen players all season.

Malcolm thinks that the players of today don't commit like they did in his day, playing with injuries week after week because of the gruelling fixtures. The pitches were shocking in those days too.

⚽

While Malcolm Macdonald was playing with Newcastle, he took part in the sports competition TV show *Superstars*, where he competed against athletes from different sports.

The show was held in Sweden in 1975. At the time, Malcolm was at his peak, playing for Newcastle, and earning around £350 per week, which he thought was a fortune.

Then he met Belgian basketball player, Willie Steveniers, who was playing in the USA, earning millions of dollars per year. He was by far the richest person Macdonald had ever met in the world of sport. It was a bit of an eye-opener.

Malcolm won the *Superstars* 100 metre sprint, in 10.9 seconds. He's been told numerous times that no other top-flight English footballer has ever run faster.

He says that he looked eleven-and-a-half stone in weight, but was actually almost fourteen stone. He was built like a tank!

⚽

In 1976, it was time for Malcolm to move on, and he joined Arsenal, for the strange fee of £333,333.34.

"Supermac" had two great seasons with "The Arsenal", and scored forty-two goals in only eighty-four appearances, which is a goal every two games.

Unfortunately, while at Arsenal, he picked up a serious knee injury in a League Cup match against Rotherham at the start of the 1978/9 season, which was to plague him for the rest of his career, and eventually lead to a dependence on alcohol to numb the constant pain.

Eventually, in the late 90s, the PFA paid for a knee operation that completely turned Malcolm's life around, and he's been teetotal ever since.

With such amazing goal-scoring ability, Malcolm should have had a great England career, but he only managed to play fourteen games for his country, scoring six goals. Five of those came in one match, in the 5-0 drubbing against Cyprus in 1975.

Malcolm's other England goal was against the World Champions at that time, West Germany.

No other player has ever scored five goals for England in a single game at Wembley, and only one other England player has ever scored five goals in one match. Willie Hall scored five goals against Ireland in 1938, but that match was played in Ireland, so "Supermac's" record looks like being around for a long, long time, don't you all agree?

Malcolm said the England manager at that time, Don Revie, who signed my schoolboy brother and myself at Leeds United, did not like him at all. He laughed and said that the real reason why Revie didn't pick him was because he always scored against Leeds, and that he was a good friend of Brian Clough, whom Revie hated with a passion.

Malcolm Macdonald finished his playing career after a short time with Swedish team, Djurgårdens IF. He was only there for a couple of months before calling it a day due to his knee problems, and he retired from playing in 1979. He was only 29 years old.

What a shame to finish such a great career so early.

Malcolm never won a major footballing honour, apart from two runners-up medals for Newcastle and one for Arsenal.

However, Malcolm was astounded when legendary football commentator John Moxon told him that he had scored a grand total of 193 goals in 381 appearances, which only one player, Jimmy Greaves, has ever bettered at the top level.

Malcolm tried managing a year after he retired in 1980, at his old club Fulham, where he had moderate success for four years. In 1987, he managed Huddersfield Town for a short time, and he retired from management in 1988.

He now lives in seclusion in the beautiful little town of Seaton Sluice, near Newcastle.

He now co-presents a football phone-in show called the Three Legends, on Community Voice FM in Middlesbrough. He also dabbles in a property business with his wife, and is an entertaining and informative after-dinner speaker.

He does go to watch Newcastle United sometimes and he is presently nursing a knee-replacement operation to match the operation sixteen years ago on his other knee.

'I did get "whacked" a lot, mainly because I was so fast,' Malcolm told me. 'But I've got no regrets at all – and good luck to the players of today who are able to earn the big money. I loved playing football at any level.'

Malcolm Macdonald's hardest opponent was, without a doubt, Derby County's Roy McFarland.

'He was an excellent "stopper". And so was his partner in crime, Colin Todd.'

I asked Malcolm about the regular "hard men" at that time, such as Tommy Smith and Ron Harris.

'Those two never really bothered me much, he laughed.

Malcolm liked all of his ex-managers equally, and admired them for different reasons.

Unfortunately, Malcolm's favourite goal was not televised. It was a goal he scored against Leicester City. He described it to me with such passion and precision. 'I hit the ball absolutely perfectly on the outside of my left foot. The ball just rocketed into the net, and the Leicester keeper had no chance whatsoever.'

Captured for posterity by television was another of Malcolm's favourite goals. He was playing for Arsenal, against Aston Villa. Malcolm hit the ball with such swerve that the ball veered almost 180 degrees in an arc.

Malcom loved scoring both of those goals very much, and remembers them as if it was yesterday.

I asked Malcolm to name the favourite club that he'd played for, and he said he had mixed feelings. He'd enjoyed all of them apart from Fulham, but he told me, with real conviction in his voice, that Arsenal really looked after their players in every way.

When Macdonald joined Arsenal, the Chairman; Denis Hill-Wood told Malcolm that the staff and officials at Arsenal would do everything within their power to make his stay a pleasant one, and that the club would do almost anything to keep him happy in every way possible.

Wood told Malcolm that the only thing that they asked of him in return was that when he went out onto the field, he should give the club 100% effort for ninety minutes, and nothing else.

Malcolm confirmed that the club was true to their word. He did say that he would have loved to play for Arsene Wenger. Everyone at Arsenal thinks they look like twins when they are together. I can't see it myself!

❦❀

One thing that Malcolm and I share is that we are both "Bow-Legged-Bastards".

We reminisced about Malcolm's old Newcastle team-mate Terry Hibberd, who was also a very bow-legged player. Sadly, he's no longer with us, but he made Malcolm a lot of goals with his great passing ability.

Terry Hibberd had previously played for Leeds, and I knew him from my early days at Leeds United, when my brother and I were invited down to Elland Road to train when we signed on as schoolboys. Terry was always swearing in training, and always moaning at everyone.

In fact, when I interviewed Eddie Gray, he brought up Terry and his bad language.

Malcolm told me about a game at Newcastle when Terry send him a long diagonal ball, and as quick as he was, Malcolm could not quite catch it. The ball just had too much pace on it.

Terry threw his hands in the air, as if to say to everyone in the ground, 'Why didn't you catch it?' Malcolm remembered the only other time this gesture had been made towards him – that time, it had been Johnnie Haynes at Fulham, and Malcolm had vowed to himself that he would never let it happen again.

When the Newcastle team came off the field and into the dressing room, Malcolm grabbed hold of Terry Hibberd by the shirt, and hung him on the coat hanger on the dressing-room door.

'Never do that to me again!' Macdonald told him.

Terry Hibberd didn't need to be told twice.

⚽

Malcolm told me an interesting story about a guy called Lenny Hepple.

Lenny was a Champion Ballroom Dancer, the father-in-law to ex-Newcastle player Pop Robson. He gave lessons in balance, and he was very good at what he did.

He always used to look at people everywhere: in the street, cafe, park; anywhere people gathered, and he could tell just by looking at them where their "Centre of Gravity" was on their body. He told Malcolm that he was the only person whom he could not help, because he said Malcolm could not be made any better.

He told him that his centre of gravity was in his penis area, which was where it should be.

When Malcolm moved to Arsenal, he met up with Lenny again because he was at Highbury to work on their centre-half, Willie Young, who was very tall and very gangly. He needed some help with his balance.

Lenny worked out that Willie's centre of gravity was around his neck area. After a short time with Lenny, Willie improved immensely. It made him a much better player for sure.

Malcolm recalls that the brilliant George Best had a great sense of balance on the pitch. Malcolm was the fastest player in the old first division, but he told me that in one game back in 1972, when Newcastle played Manchester United, a strange thing happened to him.

"Besty" was not the quickest in a race, but with a ball at his feet, he was incredibly fast. In this particular game, "Besty" had the ball and was sprinting away down the line. Malcolm set off to catch him, going like the clappers for almost seventy yards. He didn't lose George Best, but he couldn't gain an inch on him either.

'I've played against, and with, the greatest players in the game, like Beckenbauer, and Eusabio. But "Besty" was better than all of them,' Malcolm told me.

❦❂

Malcolm has no time for "diva" behaviour from footballers. We discussed fellow Tyneside heroes, such as fellow centre-forwards Jackie Milburn and Alan Shearer.

When I mentioned Shearer's name, Malcolm told me that when Shearer opened a new wing at North Tyneside Hospital, he agreed to do it on the grounds that no one could look at him or touch him during the opening ceremony. I found that quite strange, but Malcolm assured me that this information came from a good source.

❦❂

People nicknamed Malcolm Macdonald "Supermac" because he was a "super" player, and people will always remember him for his "super" speed, winning "Superstars" on TV and for scoring "super" goals.

He is simply a legend.

Malcolm and me share memories in Seaton Sluice.

CHAPTER TWENTY ONE
CHRIS WADDLE

King of the mullet,
Chris Waddle in his England
strip in the 1990 World Cup.

I got hold of Chris through David Hirst, who contacted him and confirmed that he was up for an interview.

I met Chris in his local café in Dore, Sheffield, which was very easy for me to get to.

The café filled up over lunchtime while we were talking, and it got quite busy, but we talked in depth about Chris's career.

🎱

Christopher Roland Waddle was born in Felling, Gateshead on 14 December 1960.

He played for amateur youth teams, but when he left school, he was working in a sausage factory before he started his professional playing career with Newcastle United.

He made his debut for the "Magpies" at almost twenty years old.

He told me that he'd loved his years at Newcastle and that it had been a joy to play alongside Kevin Keegan and Peter Beardsley.

Chris quickly got into his stride and became a regular in the team, which soon won promotion to the First Division in the 1983/84 season. He enjoyed playing football at Newcastle, but after five years, he decided to spread his wings, and he moved on greener pastures.

He admired the Newcastle manager, Arthur Cox. Chris said that Cox would always get that extra bit of energy out of players, by telling them that they could have done better. That made each player realise that they had more "left in the tank". Different managers have different strategies, but Chris said that he'll always have fond memories of Arthur Cox. Every player respected Arthur' decisions at Newcastle, but Chris thinks that these days, players don't have any respect at all.

Chris scored forty-six goals for Newcastle in 170 appearances.

Chris Waddle transferred to Tottenham Hotspur in 1985, for almost £600,000.

He was once again blessed, surrounded by top-class players like Clive Allen, and Glenn Hoddle, with whom he would form a close friendship.

Chris soon won the Spurs fans over with his darting runs and trickery, and it was inevitable that he would soon be called up for the full England squad. Waddle made his England debut in 1985.

He had a good England career, appearing in sixty-two games and scoring six goals.

Chris enjoyed playing for England under manager Terry Venables. He liked Venables because he would often listen to what the players had to say about certain aspects of the game. Chris said that Venables would even give the "thumbs up" to some of the ideas players had about new strategies and tactics.

'You could always tell if Terry Venables was in a good mood – he would be so jolly with his "hello". But if he was in a bad mood, he'd be totally aggressive, and you'd know to watch out!'

Chris really enjoyed his time at Spurs, and he even made a hit record with his chum Glenn Hoddle.

I know Chris and Glenn took a lot of stick for making that record, 'Diamond Lights' by "Glenn and Chris". I know how they feel.

In the 1970s, when I was playing football in Australia, I appeared on a TV talent show called "Search for a Star". I sang 'My Cherie Amour', but the week before I sang on the show, an unknown young Australian comedian appeared in the competition.

His name was Paul Hogan. At the time of his audition, he was a painter on the Sydney Harbour Bridge, but as we all know, that job didn't last very long, as he went on to star in *Crocodile Dundee* and other films.

❦❂

Chris was enjoying his football, both for Spurs and for England too.

However, there was an ambition that Chris would find impossible to fulfil in England. There was a ban on English teams playing in Europe. On 29 May 1985, the European Cup Final had been played between Liverpool and Italian club Juventus at the Heysel Stadium in Brussels. Rioting fans caused a concrete wall to collapse, and thirty-nine people, mostly Juventus fans died, and many were injured.

Chris Waddle, like so many other top English players, wanted to play at the highest level, and the only way to experience European Championship football was to play abroad.

Chris left Spurs with very fond memories, after scoring thirty-three goals, in 138 appearances.

He signed for Marseille in 1989 for £4,500,000, the third highest ever transfer fee at that time, and he soon fitted into the Marseille style of playing.

Chris told me that he loved every minute playing for Marseille, winning three French Championships straight in a row: 1990, 1991, and 1992. No one could wish for a better start than that. It's almost a fairy-tale.

One really important thing that Chris loved about Marseille's playing style was that they didn't mind him holding on to the ball, unlike the English clubs.

He loved the freedom the manager gave him to express himself, and he soon became a favourite with the Marseille fans. His consistency, week after week, earned him the nickname "Magic Chris".

Chris said that he always played well against the great AC Milan player Paolo Maldini, who was rated as one of the best full-backs in the game at the time. Chris told me that he always gave Maldini a hard time.

As well as winning a hat-trick of league titles, Chris helped to get Marseille to the final of the European Champions Cup in 1991, but his team lost on penalties to Red Star Belgrade.

Only a year earlier, Chris had missed a vital penalty for England against West Germany in the Semi-Final of the World Cup. He decided not to take a penalty against Belgrade. I didn't ask Chris about this, for obvious reasons.

In 1998, Marseille voted Chris Waddle "The Second Best ever Player of the Century". The best player was Chris' Marseille team-mate, Jean-Pierre Papin, who won the Ballon d'or in 1991.

Chris Waddle scored twenty-two goals in 107 appearances for Marseille. He told me that without a doubt, they were the best club he'd ever played for. Their style of playing suited him so much.

⚽

After three glorious seasons with Marseille, Chris decided to move back to England, and in 1992, he signed for my beloved Sheffield Wednesday. Once again, Chris found fame and glory in abundance.

The Owls paid £1,000,000 for his services, and almost every Owls fan that I know thinks that he was an absolute bargain at that price. Chris produced lots of magical moments for them, especially at Hillsborough.

He also helped to get the Owls to Wembley twice in one season, in the FA Cup Final, and the League Cup Final. Both of these finals were against Arsenal.

Unfortunately, Arsenal won both matches, but what a great year it was for the Owls, after being in the shadows for so long.

One of the great days of the 1993 season was when Wednesday played city neighbours Sheffield United, in the Semi-Final of the FA Cup at Wembley.

At that time I was living in Houston, Texas, but I just had to be back in England for that game.

I told Chris that I had arrived in London for the game early that morning, and returned to Houston on the same day, late in the evening. Now that's what you call a real fan, and that fan was me. Not only was I there, but I was also behind the goal when Chris scored that wonderful free kick from twenty yards. The stadium erupted!

Not surprisingly, Chris told me that this was his favourite all-time goal.

It was truly a great day. The moment when the final whistle went made my long journey worth it, coming across the water for the spectacle of a lifetime, seeing my boys win against the Blades.

'I loved the camaraderie at Hillsborough,' Chris told me. 'All the lads got together in the week and had a meal and a drink, probably at Hanrahan's restaurant.'

Chris loved facing the kop at Hillsborough, with the fans urging him on to do another step-over or dribble down the line.

'Sometimes when we were cruising 3-0 up, I'd dribble that extra man, when I knew I should have crossed it earlier. Brighty or Hirsty would have been waiting impatiently for the ball to come over. It's great when the fans are cheering you on to do that extra dribble, but you can't dribble all the time, you just can't!'

Chris told me that the Sheffield Wednesday team of the time could have given anyone a good game: 'There was such a great balance in the team, especially in midfield, with John Sheridan, Carlton Palmer, John Harkes – and me!'

Chris had four good years at Hillsborough, and was voted "Player of the Year" by the Football Writers' Association in 1993.

In 109 appearances for Sheffield Wednesday, Chris Waddle scored ten goals.

Chris thought that after his amazing season with the Owls in 1992/93, and his "Player of the Year" accolade, he might get another England call-up, but it wasn't to be. Chris says that he's never borne any malice about England Manager Graham Taylor's decision not to pick him for the national team.

'He was the manager, and it's up to him who he picks. It's all about opinions, just like I have mine,' Chris shrugged.

Chris' favourite matches with Sheffield Wednesday were the derby games against the Blades, especially that magical semi-final at Wembley.

The atmosphere of the games between the two Sheffield sides reminded Chris of the matches between Marseille and Paris Saint-Germain, even though the two French teams were located at opposite ends of the country.

In 1996, Chris moved much further up north, for a season with Falkirk. Howard Wilkinson had been keen for Chris to play for Leeds, and had offered him a lot more money than he'd been earning at Hillsborough. However, Chris didn't like the way that Leeds played, so he opted to play in Scotland. He didn't stay there long, though, playing in only four games and scoring just one goal.

Chris then signed for Bradford City in 1996, scoring six goals in twenty-five appearances. One goal was quite memorable to him: when he scored against Everton in the FA Cup at Goodison Park. 'I scored a great goal that day.'

In 1997, he moved again to Sunderland, but only stayed for part of the season, playing in just seven games and scoring one goal. Chris then moved to Burnley, where he played thirty-two games, again scoring just the one goal.

Chris' last club in the football league was Torquay United in 1998. He only lasted seven games, before retiring from playing full-time that same year.

๕๑

I asked Chris if he had any regrets:

'None at all, Norm, especially for a lad who was working in a sausage factory.' I loved that reply. 'I played sixty-two times for England. I would definitely say "no regrets". Wouldn't you?'

Chris told me that wherever he went, he'd always enjoyed playing football, and that he always checked out each club he was joining first to find out how they played. That's what put him off signing for Leeds United – he didn't like their playing style.

Chris didn't score many goals throughout his long career, but he did score some "beauties", such as the goal against the Blades at that famous Wembley game, and also his goal against Everton, playing for Bradford City. Chris also talked about a special goal he'd scored when playing for Marseille – so take your pick!

His favourite manager was Terry Venables, but he said that everywhere he played, he'd had a good understanding with the manager.

The hardest opponent Chris Waddle ever played against was Kenny Samson. 'When I would try to go past him, he would always nick the ball off you with a toe poke. He was great at reading "One on one" situations.'

I had a feeling that when I asked Chris to name his favourite player of all time, he would mention another winger like himself. Chris loves the art of dribbling, and he's really passionate about the English game needing more dribblers.

I have to agree with Chris on this point. I'm fed up of watching England play with no wingers or strikers willing to take the defenders on.

'It's all pass, pass, pass,' Chris said. 'They've coached dribbling out of football now. All they want is for the players to pass and run at 100mph, and that's what's wrong with the English game.'

I agree with him entirely – it's so boring and negative watching our national team play.

I was right about Chris's all-time favourite player being a winger – the footballer he most admires is the brilliant Brazilian winger Manuel Francisco dos Santos, known as "Garrincha", which means "Little Bird", who is regarded as the best dribbler in football history.

Chris adores watching footage of Garrincha playing, and loves the way he used to dribble past the defenders on both sides of the pitch.

Glenn Hoddle was the best footballer that Chris ever played with (attempted pop careers aside!) 'He was brilliant with the ball, and his vision was next to none.'

⚽

Chris is 100% correct about the way our game is being coached.

We both agreed that great teams like the Barcelona of today also pass the ball a lot, but then someone like Messi will then dribble directly past two or three defenders. However, the England team doesn't do that, and doesn't have the players with the skills to do that.

Chris loves Messi, but he wonders who is going to take his crown, because he just doesn't see anyone else with the ability to do what Messi does on a regular basis.

Kids love to watch dribblers, just as much as adults do, because it creates excitement, and we need that excitement in the English game.

I know everyone thinks the Premier League is the best in the world, but all the best players in it are foreigners.

Chris agrees – he thinks the Premiership is overrated, and too hyped up.

He said that it just doesn't excite him anymore. He told me that he couldn't name five players who hold his attention. He gets p*ssed off by people who describe players as "world class", when they're just good.

Chris thinks that the Premier League players don't have as much skill as the media makes out. 'Walcott and Navas go past players, but not by skill – only because they have great pace.'

He said that he was never taught to pass all the time, but to express himself and dribble as much as possible. When Chris was growing up, he was a big fan of Aston Villa winger Tony Morley, but he was told to watch Nottingham Forest winger John Robertson, because he would learn more from watching – Robertson had natural skill, not just speed.

However, we agreed that it's good that the referees in the Premier League don't allow as much kicking going on towards the forwards, so it's an ideal climate for mid-fielders to take players on more often in those danger areas.

Players like Zlatan Ibrahimović of Paris Saint-Germain have great skills, but the Premiership would be too quick for him. It's all about speed, and that's why players like him just wouldn't be able to cut it in the Premiership.

Chris thinks that we need more exciting players, like George Best, Rodney Marsh, John Robertson, Glenn Hoddle and Tommy Hutchinson, and crowd-pleasers, such as Frank Worthington.

When you take a look at academies in the Premier League, they have just as many foreign youngsters as they do English. So how do we improve our English team, when there's only one "Gazza" or Rooney that comes along every ten years or so?

We also both agreed that Arsene Wenger of Arsenal has the right idea, by encouraging playing with skill, and not just runners. Quite simply, he prefers quality rather than quantity. How many Jack Wilsheres are there in the Premier, willing to take on defenders time after time?

We also agreed that this season Liverpool have a great balance and that they are really exciting at times when going forward.

Chris thinks that English players train too hard and that they should rest more, instead of running and training all the time. That makes a lot of sense, because after watching England play against Denmark on home soil, they need to vastly improve.

I really liked Chris' insight into the English game and the Premier League. He was certainly enjoyable to interview, especially because he tells it how it is. I have always liked people who aren't scared to say what they think.

In 2013, Chris Waddle told BBC Radio 5 Live that David Beckham wouldn't get into his top 1,000 of the best players from the past forty years. Chris said that Beckham was a good player, but not a great one.

That's enough about Mr Beckham for now.

Personally, I think that Chris Waddle was truly a great player. Not just because he graced the Hillsborough turf for four years, but purely based on what I saw of him myself.

Trust me, I'm not the only one who admires Chris Waddle's playing. Great players like him are sadly missed, both on the domestic terraces and in the international stadiums.

Chris Waddle and me, putting the world of modern football to rights.

CHAPTER TWENTY TWO
PHILIP SCORTHORNE

Norm and Phil Scorthorne run in the first Sheffield Marathon in 1982. We're the good-looking lads with moustaches in the top right-hand corner!

I've known Phil Scorthorne since we were both at school.

We played against each other: I was playing for the Jordanthorpe under-14s team, and Phil was at Tapton.

Tapton beat us at home 1-2, which was the only game our team had lost in over three years, but later, we had our revenge when we played at Tapton's ground.

I remember it like it was yesterday. We were 5-3 down at half-time, but finished up winning 5-9, with my brother Maurice scoring five goals.

Phil and I shook hands after both games, and we bonded as friends. We've been great mates ever since.

We arranged to meet for our interview at lunchtime at the firm Phil runs, and it was laughs all the way.

Philip "Scony" Scorthorne was born in Sheffield on 13 May, 1950.

When I met Phil as a schoolboy player, our teams had a keen rivalry. We had some good battles with Tapton, with Jordanthorpe just about managing to get the better of them.

I could see then that Phil was going to be a very good player in the future, and also his team-mate Mick Daley showed a lot of promise.

Over the years, Phil and I gradually lost contact, but we've always had a great mutual respect for each other, not only in football, but as friends.

I was lucky enough to play and coach abroad in Australia, Malta, Hong Kong, America, Brazil, Philippines, and of course my native England, but Phil and I have always found time for each other in one way or another.

Phil's personality will light up any room. He's a great guy to go out with, and I would recommend a night on the town with our Scony anytime.

Phil's playing career after school started at his local Crookes team, The Ball, where he was spotted by a Sheffield Wednesday official and asked if he would like to have a trial with them. Obviously Phil agreed, and soon enough, he was down at Hillsborough with his boots across his shoulders, waiting to show the Owls what he could do on the pitch.

He was just seventeen at the time, so the opportunity came at just the right time for him.

The funny thing was that Phil thought he would be playing in the under nineteen's team, but they had no room for him at that particular time. They told him that he would be playing in the reserves against the mighty Liverpool.

When Phil heard this news, he practically sh*t himself, but at the same time, he was very excited. Let's face it! If you're going to try to impress someone, why not do it against the best, and that's just what Phil did.

For a young lad of seventeen, coming into a big team at reserve team level was an achievement in itself, but to hold your own against the might of Liverpool was remarkable by any standards.

Ten minutes from the end, the coach brought Phil off. He went to the side-lines, where an oldish guy told him that he was sitting in the wrong dug-out, just like Ron Atkinson did in his first game as manager for Nottingham Forest!

Phil said that he couldn't understand the guy's accent at all, and it turned out to be none other than the legendary

Liverpool manager Bob Paisley. As Phil told me the story, I was laughing my b*ll*cks off!

Phil told me that Sheffield Wednesday didn't sign him after all, and so he went on trial with Derby County, with another well-known manager, Brian Clough.

Nothing developed there either, so Phil signed with Yorkshire League team Dinnington, where he prospered for a couple of years, putting in good performances, week-by-week.

Offers came from better teams in higher leagues, and one of them was Matlock Town. Phil was still only twenty years old, so to play in the Northern Premier was a big move up for him.

Matlock's manager at the time was my old mate Ian Swift, who signed me for Heanor Town many years ago. Ian was a great guy and I liked playing for him. I also remembered Ian's lady friend at the time, who had an enormous beehive hairdo. Phil and I had a really good laugh, remembering it.

Phil played about twelve games with Matlock Town on the right wing, and played well, but then Matlock told him they couldn't sign him because they had to cut the wage bill.

As a result, Phil was on his travels once again.

He then had short spells at Ashby and also at Retford but he wasn't totally happy with either club, so he then had a chance to play with Frickley Colliery, where he had his finest scoring record to date.

Phil played on the right wing in his usual position, where he was known for being quick and a great crosser of the ball.

However, in his short time at Frickley, he managed to bang home thirty goals in one season, which was a brilliant feat for a winger at any level.

'I still can't f*cking believe it, Norm. I scored thirty goals in a season. I'm usually lucky if I score three,' Phil joked.

Phil's greatest achievement when he was playing for Frickley was when he scored two goals against Rhyl in the FA Cup. It was televised on Match of the Day. Phil told me that the fans were calling him a George Best lookalike, with his long black floppy hair and his trickery on the wing. All I could think of was 'that's my boy Scony.'

An old friend of mine, Ray Elliott once took me to Frickley when Phil was playing there. I was really surprised that Phil also knew him and had played with him. It was a big shock to find out that Ray had been killed in a car crash a few years ago. Ray was a real character too.

⚽

Phil enjoyed his stay at Frickley, but his best years were still to come, when he joined Boston Town at the age of twenty three. He played for them for almost ten seasons, which at that time was a club record. Phil put in 303 appearances for the Lincolnshire team.

He really loved playing for Boston, enjoying every season, and having the luxury of playing with some of his Sheffield mates too.

Phil's best mate there was my old friend Dennis Beatson, who sadly passed away a while ago. Boston released Dennis after a few years of them playing together, and after that, Boston Town wasn't quite as special any more.

One Boston memory that will always stick in Phil's head is when they played away at Barnsley in the first round of the FA Cup. Boston scored first, with a goal from my old mate Mick Daley.

Barnsley eventually won the game 3-1, but it was still a great day for Boston. That was the favourite game of Phil's career.

Phil said that he'd played against some good defenders, but his hardest opponent had been ex-Nottingham Forest and Scotland player Kenny Burns. Phil said that Kenny was always one step ahead of everybody else.

Phil's favourite goal was when he was playing for Boston against Bangor. 'It was a beauty,' he said. 'I remember it like it was yesterday.'

We discussed our favourite players of all time. Mine is Diego Maradona – a true genius with a ball, and Phil's choice was Kenny Dalglish. However, when he was younger, he favoured Jimmy Greenhoff.

Phil's fondest memories were obviously from his time with Boston. He only has great memories of playing for them, apart from when I scored against them for Skegness Town.

⚽

After leaving Boston, Phil had a brief spell with Eastwood, but moved on fairly soon.

Phil was now approaching his thirty second birthday. His final fling in football was at his very own local club, Crookes, which was being run by Danny Hague and my old pal from Sheffield United, Dave Staniforth. Phil played for them for a while, but he wasn't living in Sheffield at the time and he got fed up of travelling. He decided to retire gracefully.

Phil's Brother Steve played many years for Crookes, and he was as good a striker as anyone I know, but Phil said that he just wasn't bothered about playing at a higher level. He was a talented goal-scorer though. I always rated him highly.

⚽

Now retired from playing, Phil runs a successful engineering company with his business partner David, whom I happened to bump into at our gym a while ago.

Phil keeps in trim by still playing five-a-side football every week. He still looks fit, and is probably giving the youngsters something to remember him by.

He told me that he's going to retire to Portugal, so I guess I should be okay for a free holiday sometime in the near future.

Another great memory of Phil and me was when we ran the very first full Sheffield Marathon together in 1980, with Tony Orlando lookalike Tony Hughes.

I have to tell everyone here the truth about a certain incident during the race. The three of us were on the eighteenth mile, almost totally exhausted, when out of nowhere came a pensioner, about seventy five years old. He sprinted past the three of us with such ease. We just couldn't believe it. Bear in mind that the three of us were fit footballers at that time, with an average age of thirty years old. We all stared in amazement as the old guy flew past us.

I don't think any of us will ever live that down.

We finished the whole marathon in over four hours, but none of us had really trained for it seriously. Phil and I have some great memories from that first ever Sheffield Marathon, but we never ran any more marathons together.

However, after that, I got the "bug", running more marathons for charities, and managing much better times. I even ran the whole of the Sheffield Marathon in bare feet once; the whole twenty-six miles. I must have been crazy. The things you do for charity!

Phil told me that he had tried to contact me for his wedding a couple of years ago, but he just couldn't get hold of my whereabouts. Like I said earlier, sometimes we lose contact, but our friendship has never faded.

I always look back with fond memories of past meetings. Once, I had just come back from America, and I was having a drink with some mates in the Sheffield wine bar Hanrahans, standing near the stairs.

All of a sudden, something crashed down on me, and I heard the words: 'Parkino! Where the f*ck have you been hiding?'

It was Phil doing a dive bomb on the top of my head, crushing me into oblivion. People say I'm crazy, but Scony is definitely in that category.

Every time we meet, we always have great warmth for each other. I can truly say that it will continue to be so, because even though we have each had contrasting football careers, there has never been any jealousy or envy between us at all. We've always loved hearing about the latest thing the other has done or achieved.

Personally, I think that Phil could have played at an even higher level than he did. He had great ability, and he had one ingredient that all forwards need: speed.

The only time I beat him in a race was when I caught the bus!

When I told Phil that I was writing a book about my favourite ex-footballers and characters, he just laughed and said that I should write more about my own exploits and call the book *Fifty Shades of Parkin*.

I think Phil Scorthorne deserves to be in this book for two main reasons.

Firstly, because I wanted to interview a player who has had a great career even if it hasn't been at the top flight. However, I always thought that he should have been playing at the top level, so that gives him the right to be amongst those other great players.

Secondly, because I just admire Phil as a human being, and I will always treasure the friendship I have with him.

To finish my chapter on Phil, I will mention that a few weeks ago, Phil sent me a message on Facebook.

It simply said: 'Do you know, Norm, that we have been friends for over fifty years and we've never fallen out or argued once. Isn't that great?'

That one statement says everything. Phil Scorthorne is a legend in every sense of the word, in football and as a person.

Friends Reunited: me and Phil.

CHAPTER TWENTY THREE
JÜRGEN GRABOWSKI

Jürgen Grabowski playing
for Eintracht Frankfurt.

Back in 1978, I played against the great West German team German Eintracht Frankfurt. Their star player was Jürgen Grabowski, and we swapped shirts after the game.

The main reason why I wanted to put Jürgen in my book is simply because he is the best player I have ever played against in a professional game.

🔴⚽

In the 1977/78 season, I was playing for Sliema Wanderers of Malta. We were drawn against the mighty German Team Eintracht Frankfurt in the first round of the UEFA Cup. It was a two-legged tie, with the first leg of the match being played in Frankfurt.

The prospect of facing the German team on their home ground was scary to say the least. I can remember some of my team-mates being very nervous the night before the match.

In an attempt to unwind, we all went downtown in Frankfurt for the evening, and started to relax. Until yours truly stumbled upon the "red light" district, with German ladies of the night in shop windows, touting for business.

I will never forget the look on some of our players' faces; they looked so shocked. I guess that living in a small Catholic community like Malta would be quite different from the bright lights of Frankfurt.

The day before, we had played a friendly game against German second division team, VFL Neustadt. I'm pleased to say that I scored the opening goal in the sixty-fourth minute with a cracker just inside the box, but Neustadt equalized five minutes later, and the final result was 1-1.

I remember saying to the guys how disappointing the Neustadt team was for a top second-division team playing in their own back yard. They didn't really offer much threat at all.

In fact, we should have taken the lead again right at the end, and I'm sorry to say it was me who missed a good chance, scuffing the ball wide. To be fair to our guys, we did play very well and we were buzzing with confidence and excitement about the big game soon to be upon us.

We shouldn't have been so complacent. Grabowski and his team were in a different class from beginning to end, showing their class and style throughout the game. Nevertheless, it was a great experience to play against such a talented team and in front of a big German crowd too.

We lost 5-0, and to be honest, we were totally out-played, as to be expected. I played a very lonely role upfront that night, and I hardly got a kick in the first half.

After the game in Germany, the Frankfurt officials gave every member of our team a gold-plated cufflink set, in a suede box with the Eintracht badge on them, which I still have today.

⚽

The return leg in Malta was a completely different story. We tied 0-0, but we should have won the game by at least two goals.

I hit the bar with a good header, and we were very unlucky not to get a result, but I guess the Germans had done enough to go through with their great performance in the first game.

A player who really impressed me in our first meeting with Frankfurt was Bernd Nickel. He was a German international and possessed a ferocious shot, earning him the nickname 'Doktor Hammer'.

Nickel was a real thorn in our side for most of the game, but it was the sheer class and guile from Jürgen Grabowski that really caught my eye and made me realise what a great player he really was. He seemed to have so much time on the ball, and was one step ahead of everybody in his thinking and vision.

Eintracht Frankfurt was full of German international players, and another name that comes to mind was their centre-forward, Bernd Hölzenbein, who was very influential throughout the game.

The second game was not as memorable to me, even though we played much better and managed to tie with them, but they will always be the two favourite games that I ever played in. To top everything, I even swapped shirts with Grabowski after the match. I still treasure it.

My friends often joke about putting Grabowski's shirt on eBay but I would never sell it.

1977: my header against Eintracht Frankfurt hits the woodwork.

Jürgen Grabowski was born on 7 July, 1944, in Wiesbaden, Germany.

He joined his first professional football club, local team FV Biebrich, in 1960. He played with the team until 1965, before moving onto one of Germany's biggest clubs, Eintracht Frankfurt.

Jürgen had a great career at Frankfurt, starting as a forward and also having the ability to play on either flank. Later in his career, he moved into midfield where he was just as effective.

Jürgen played 441 games for Frankfurt and scored 109 goals.

He helped Frankfurt to win the German Cup twice, in 1973/74 and in 1974/75.

Eintracht Frankfurt also won the UEFA Cup in 1980, playing against another German team Borussia Mönchengladbach in the final.

Jürgen Grabowski played forty-four games for West Germany, and scored five goals. He was a member of the West German

World Cup Squad in 1966, but he didn't play in any matches. However, he did play in the World Cups of 1970 and 1974.

He played his last game for Frankfurt in 1980, when he was badly injured by another famous German international player, Lother Matthäus, who had then just started his career at Borussia Mönchengladbach.

Grabowski had a wonderful career with Eintracht Frankfurt and Germany, and I'm sure he will be remembered for a long time by Frankfurt fans.

He now sometimes writes football articles in the German newspapers and commentates on German football, but he says that his main hobby is getting on the golf course as often as he can.

⚽

I have left this story until last. I still find it hard to believe that it actually happened.

My friend and colleague, Leo Jensen asked me to come over to his house a few months ago because he had a surprise for me.

I told him that I would come over, but he also stressed that I had to be there for midday, and he emphasised that I must not be late.

I was getting rather excited about what the surprise was – I really had no idea, but Leo is always full of surprises in one way or another.

When we arrived, Leo told me to sit down and wait by the phone, and my surprise would be complete. The phone rang almost bang-on twelve o clock, and Leo answered it.

He was talking loudly, as if the phone call came from far away. In actual fact, it came from Germany. Frankfurt to be precise. None other than Jürgen Grabowski was on the other end of the phone, calling to speak to me.

I just could not believe it. I was completely flabbergasted. I just had no idea that Jürgen Grabowski was calling me. It was thirty-seven years since we'd last seen each other on a football pitch.

It was a moment that I will never forget, and it was all down to my dear wonderful friend, Leo "Beauwolf" Jensen, for setting it all up and making it happen. I will be in his debt forever.

We had a little language problem at first, but we managed to get by, and I mentioned to him that I still had his shirt that he'd swapped with me after the game. Jürgen joked, saying he hoped I'd kept it clean!

I asked Jürgen to name the favourite game he'd ever played in. He didn't hesitate. It was obviously the 1974 World Cup final between West Germany and Holland, which the Germans won 2-1.

Jürgen's second favourite game was when West Germany played England in the 1970 World Cup in Mexico, with the Germans winning 3-2 in extra time.

He had no doubts about choosing his favourite all-time player. It's Pelé.

The favourite goal that Jürgen ever scored was when he was playing for West Germany against Sweden in the 1974 World Cup in Germany.

I also wanted to know who his most difficult opponent was and he answered right away: Berti Vogts of Borrusia Monchengladbach.

As most of you football fans out there know, Mr Grabowski was an excellent dribbler down wings, left or right, but he said that Vogts was so hard to get past that he was really difficult to play against.

Jürgen also mentioned that another difficult opponent was Rudi Krol of Holland, because he always gave him problems.

Jürgen was keen to answer every question I asked him. My next question was always going to be a little predictable. I asked him to name his greatest ever achievement. Of course it was always going to be winning the 1974 World Cup final against Holland.

How can anyone beat that in a career of football? It is surely the pinnacle of any professional footballers' life.

Jürgen's fondest ever moment in football was in 1974, when the referee blew his full-time whistle, making West Germany the World Champions.

⚽

As you can see, Jürgen Grabowski has had some great highs, and not too many lows in his career, playing in some great, memorable games for his club and for his country.

He did say that the only thing that he regretted was that he thought he'd retired from international football too early. However, he was happy with his decision to stop playing.

I also asked Jürgen what he thought about the game today. He said he thought that football has become so popular these days that it is by far the most important game in the world. Football has brought the world's media with it in every way.

We discussed the games we played against each other as best as we could. Jürgen also told me about the football journalism he does nowadays. Just to have him on the other end of the phone was a sheer delight.

I will always love Leo for setting up my meeting with Jürgen Grabowski. I will be forever grateful to him.

⚽

To add to the memory of the game against Frankfurt, I have still got the poster advertising the game in Germany hanging in my lounge.

The poster: pride of place in my lounge.

Little does anyone know that the poster was hanging in our hotel in Frankfurt, advertising the game, like they usually do in England.

I had to fight off at least three other players from my team while I was taking the poster off the hotel wall, but in the end I got it, as you can see by this photograph.

⚽

Well, I never played against Archie Gemmill, Eddie Gray or Malcolm Macdonald, but I did play against Bernd Nickel, Bernd Holzenbein, and the main man, Jürgen Grabowski. After all, playing against the top First Division team in Germany, Eintracht Frankfurt, was the equivalent of playing against Manchester United or Chelsea by any standards.

It was a wonderful experience for me to play in both games, home and away, and if only my header in the second game had gone in, instead of hitting the bar, it would have been a memory to really treasure, scoring the winning goal in the home leg of the match.

I will always remember those two games as long as I have a memory. Take care, Jürgen Grabowski – a truly great player in every sense of the word.

Jürgen Grabowski,
remembering his
amazing footballing
achievements.

Me in 1977, treasuring
Grabowski's shirt.

CHAPTER TWENTY FOUR
PARKIN'S OBSERVATIONS

A man of many opinions...

If there's one thing that every football player or fan has in common, it's that everyone has their own strong opinions on the game.

No matter what aspect of football is being discussed, be it players, managers, transfers or referees, football must be the most controversial and talked about sport in the world, for lots of different reasons.

I need to explain that what you are about to read is simply my own opinions on certain issues and players.

That's why I have called this chapter 'Parkin's Observations', because that is what they are, pure and simple. These are just my own observations on certain issues and certain people, but they are by no means what everyone else thinks.

The most common subject that football fans everywhere seem to talk about, usually critically, is the amount of money that the players earn these days.

I don't know what all the fuss is about, personally. The game has changed so much and so rapidly that it is hard to make comparisons.

I know that when I was playing many years ago, wages were nothing like nowadays, but it's not the players' fault. When I was playing, there was no Sky television, promoting the game to a level of excellence and exposure never seen before.

Sooner or later, the teams were bound to start competing for players by paying ever increasing wages, and the players of today are reaping the benefits. Good luck to them, I say.

In my day, players did not have agents who did everything for them.

The majority of Premier League clubs in England are now being taken over by foreign owners. The reason for the clubs letting them in is simply because they put lots of cash into the club. Look at the wages bill at Manchester City – it's phenomenal! Just like Paris Saint-Germain, both teams are buying new players without any thought of the asking price, because they have the money to buy anyone.

It has affected the game for sure, and with the greedy ten-percent agents hovering around like vultures, squeezing clubs for every last penny that they can get out of them, the inevitable was bound to happen.

Don't get me wrong, it really is wonderful watching all these great, mostly foreign, players every week in the "Premiership", but it has a price.

Yes! I love England having the best league in the world on my doorstep, but because of the Premiership's popularity amongst the top foreign players, it means that our home-grown talent doesn't get the chance to play top-flight football.

Because "Joe Bloggs" from Africa is on a contract of £100,000 a week for example, his club is more or less committed to play him, which leaves our young hopefuls stuck in the reserves unless they are a really special talent, like Luke Shaw or Raheem Sterling.

⚽

One issue that does p*ss me off sometimes is the new rules and laws of the game.

I admit that I really love the "no pass back to the keeper" rule, because that keeps the game flowing, and it creates awareness in sticky situations.

One new rule I hate is the "foul from the last defender with goal scoring opportunity for the striker".

There have been so many different interpretations of that rule that it is a complete joke. It should be abolished immediately, because it makes certain officials look stupid, and it is quite clear to see that everyone involved in football really does not like it at all. It really is a bad rule.

Another issue in football that really needs to be addressed as soon as possible is corruption in the game.

I'm sorry to say this, but corruption is growing rapidly. It's not just in other countries, it's here in Britain too.

We've had a small taste of it in the past, with certain managers being accused of taking a "bung", but now it's on the move again and needs to be stamped out completely. Also recently, players with English clubs have been match-fixing and some of them have been arrested, just like in Italy and Ghana not so long ago.

To top everything, there is now corruption at the very highest order in football. This involves FIFA and their main man, Sepp Blatter.

I met Mr Blatter in 2007, at the inauguration of my dear friend and colleague, Mari Martinez, as the new President of the Philippine Football Federation.

Sepp Blatter came across as an unassuming, humble person, but people change in walks of life all the time, and I think, just like a lot of other people, that Mr Blatter has a few questions to answer, especially around allegations of bribery relating to Qatar's successful 2022 World Cup bid.

Anyhow, I don't want to dwell on negativity about the bad side of football, so let me tell you some of my thoughts, memories and observations about the past, present and future of our beautiful game that spring to mind.

I'm sure I will have missed a few, but certain memories will never fade.

There are some great teams that come to my mind without any prompting, like the brilliant Celtic team that won the European Cup against Inter Milan in 1967.

The team included great players, like Jimmy Johnson, Bobby Lennox and Tommy Gemmell, just to name a few. I loved watching Jimmy Johnson tear down the wing, frightening defenders with his pace.

That's the team that Eddie Gray and I talked about, when he told me that not only were all the Celtic players Scottish, they were all from Glasgow.

I find that amazing: to have found success at the highest level in Europe with eleven local players is a really incredible achievement.

Nottingham Forest also had a great team, and also had great success in Europe, winning the European Cup twice back-to-back, in 1979 against Malmo, and in 1980 against Hamburg.

I loved the Notts Forest team that "Cloughie" put together with Peter Taylor. What a lot of people never realised was that it wasn't Brian Clough who found all those great players, but his side-kick, Peter Taylor. He never got the recognition that he should have. He was great at spying new talent; he just had a knack for it.

"Cloughie" also found a few players for the team, but his gift was motivating his team, and man-management. They too had all-British players, but a mixture of English, Scottish and Irish.

The classic Nottingham Forest squad had players including Peter Shilton, Trevor Francis, Tony Woodcock and my favourite, John Robertson. I'd better mention Kenny Burns too, because he's in this book. I wouldn't like to upset Kenny, because he was one of my best interviewees. We didn't stop laughing from beginning to end. Besides that, he was a great player, upfront or in defence.

Another favourite team of mine was the 1970 Brazilian World Cup team. They had great players in every department, from Carlos Alberto (who I met in Texas at a coaching seminar), Rivellino, Jairzinho, Tostão, and of course, Pelé, but the one player I thought was magnificent throughout the tournament, who hardly gets a mention, was Gerson. I thought he was real quality.

I would also like to comment on how much pleasure Bobby Robson's Ipswich team gave me back in the early eighties. Wonderful players like the two Dutchmen Arnold Mühren and Frans Thijssen; two lovely footballers, and Clive Woods, Alan Brazil, Eric Gates, and John Wark, another underrated player who, for a midfield player, scored remarkable goals, season after season. Mr Robson really had a great team at that moment in time. They were a joy to watch.

I have to also mention the great Arsenal team of 2003/4, which went through an entire season without losing a single game. They had a great team of gifted players like Robert Pirès, Patrick Vieira, Dennis Bergkamp, Silvain Wiltord, and of course, Thierry Henry.

I honestly don't think that a team will ever win matches again so consistently in the Premiership. It was a marvellous achievement by any standards. Manchester City won the Premiership title this year, with Chelsea and Liverpool both hot on their heels, but all three teams lost six games through the season. I seriously can't imagine any team winning every match again, not in my lifetime.

I've always loved the Dutch teams, old and new. For me, Holland is always the best team to watch at an international level.

They play with such style and without fear. Back in the days of Johan Cruyff, when they played their so called "total football", they were great to watch, but sadly they never won the biggest event, the World Cup. They came so close.

When a team has as much ability in it, like Johnny Rep, René and Willy Van de Kerkhof, Ruud Krol, Robbie Rensenbrink, Johan Neeskens and the brilliant Johan Cruyff, you would think that they would clean up, so to speak, but alas! It was not so.

As we all know from the history books, it's not always the team with the best players that wins.

I know some of you will wonder why I haven't mentioned certain other teams, but the ones I have mentioned here are just a few that are already lodged in my head. Otherwise, I would never finish this chapter, would I?

⚽

The last great team I will mention has a real sadness to it, because I'm talking about the wonderfully gifted "Busby Babes" of Manchester United.

Matt Busby groomed these kids for stardom in the late fifties, and who knows what they would have achieved if that terrible accident had never happened. They really were special, with an average age of around nineteen or twenty, and they had talent throughout the team.

When a team loses a couple of players, things can usually be put right, but when a team loses eight players, then there is no quick solution. There were eight fatalities in the crash, but another five players had been seriously injured.

Manchester United struggled to cope with the aftermath of the accident, but they carried on with their domestic games for the rest of the season, and Matt Busby ultimately built a second generation of Busby Babes, with George Best included in the line-up.

On February 6, 1958, the football world was robbed of immense talent. I think it has to be the saddest day ever in British football.

⚽

This chapter wouldn't be complete without a section about our great heritage of British football managers. These days, they seem to have no personality, and they don't seem to stay very long at one club. That's not necessarily by any fault of their own.

Football is a cut-throat business, and the club owners want success quickly and are not prepared to wait very long for it, generally speaking. Like I said earlier, these new mega-rich owners expect results, and if they don't get them, they will change the manager, just like Manchester United has recently done with David Moyes.

Moyes did not become a bad manager overnight. However, United's owners didn't want to risk giving Mr Moyes millions of pounds to buy the wrong players and finish up missing out on the Champions league again.

You have to see their side of the coin, especially when the team were crowned champions only the year before, but had slipped to finishing seventh this year. The manager had to go.

I really miss the managers who had character as well as quality, like Bill Shankly of Liverpool. I don't think I know of any other manager who came out with as many brilliant one-liners as he did.

When he was asked who the two best teams in England were, he replied: 'The best team is Liverpool, and the second best team is Liverpool reserves.' I just loved that man's wit.

He was a great manager too, and he will never be forgotten for what he did at Liverpool. Shankly had charisma in abundance.

In comparison, another great Liverpool manager Bob Paisley was never loved in the same way as Bill Shankly, maybe because he was just "the guy next door", but if you compare the success that each of them had with Liverpool, Paisley actually wins by a mile. His record at 'Anfield' is phenomenal.

Tommy Docherty was another manager with a sharp wit, and a character to go with it. I remember when he was manager of little Rotherham United in the late 60s, and he told everyone that he would take them out of the second division. He did: they were relegated to the third.

He was a manager who was always in the news, whether it was good or bad. I think that people had a love or hate relationship with "The Doc".

I, for one, was in his fan club, because I loved his dry humour and his no-nonsense attitude towards people he didn't like. I have to say that sometimes he did speak before thinking, but nevertheless, the "Doc" is sorely missed from the world of football management, well at least by me he is.

Love him or hate him, you have to admit that the game needs characters like Tommy Docherty.

⚽

I want to make it quite clear that I'm not just mentioning this next character because he's in this book, but because I sincerely believe that he is sadly missed in the game. I'm talking about "Big Ron" Atkinson.

When I interviewed Ron a few months ago, he was as vibrant as ever: joking all the time, smiling and messing around in a jovial way.

I really think it's a crying shame that he's not managing a team, especially with the lack of good English managers around at the moment, when "Big Ron" is still as active as ever, physically and mentally.

I asked him about getting back in the game as a manager, and he just kind of shrugged his shoulders, as if to say that nobody wanted him.

I even hinted with my tongue in my cheek, about him joining the "Owls" again, because the "Wednesdayites" love him, and I will say this with my hand on my heart, that I still wish he was at the helm at Sheffield Wednesday. Not only me, but hundreds of other "Owls" fans would welcome him back with open arms.

Ron Atkinson was born to be on the "centre stage". It suits him down to a tee. I still think it was ridiculous what happened to him because of his infamous "off air" comment about Chelsea's Marcel Desailly. I think it was very harsh to put Atkinson in virtual exile from football for one badly-judged comment.

I would personally love to see him managing a team in the Premiership, and I think a lot of other people would love that too. Even now, he would make an impact. The game needs "Big Ron".

⚽

I can't write about past managers without giving "Old Bighead" a mention, can I? Of course I'm talking about the one and only Brian Clough.

What a character Mr Clough was. I know he had his faults, but I would like to think that most people who remembered him would put him in the category of being a true legend in every sense of the word. Not only for his great ability as a manager, but also for being the extraordinary character that he was.

I have got one or two characters right here in this book, but none of them come close to Brian Clough.

In my opinion, there has never been a football manager like him.

Brian Clough brought a new dimension to the game with his outrageous remarks and spontaneous answers.

He was as sharp as he once was on the football field. Most people don't even realise what a great striker he was when he played with Middlesbrough, and Sunderland. He played in 274 games and scored 251 goals, which was remarkable by any standards.

He was the complete manager, and it would have been wonderful if the English FA had been brave enough to make him manager of England. Then we might have stood a chance of winning a trophy or two with our national team. It does have to be said, though, that he was never a real success without Peter Taylor, as I mentioned earlier in the book.

You only have to remember that when he joined Leeds United after Don Revie left, he was totally lost without Peter Taylor.

It was really obvious that Revie and Clough didn't like each other very much, but they did respect each other's achievements, which were plain to see. What was ironic was that they grew up practically in the same neighbourhood in Middlesbrough.

I knew Don Revie, because he signed me and my brother for Leeds United many years ago while we were still schoolboys at Jordanthorpe Secondary school in Sheffield. Sometimes, during the school holidays, Mr Revie would invite the two of us down to Leeds to train with the young apprentices.

One story, which I know to be true, from a very good source, was when Brian Clough first joined Leeds and he was meeting all the first team players.

He told them that they were a great team, but that they had won everything by cheating, so they could throw all their cups and trophies in the f*cking bin, because now they were going to win them fair and square without being the dirty b*st*rds that they were before.

That was "Cloughie": straight to the point. I have to say that I sadly miss him on the touch line and in the television studio, because we need his kind of character in our wonderful game.

Having said that, my old mate Neil Warnock is now back where he belongs, managing Crystal Palace again, and I'm hoping that it works out well.

I know that Neil upsets certain people with his blunt comments, but he also gives a lot of pleasure too.

One thing about Neil is that he shoots from the hip and lets you know exactly how it is.

The game is far better off with Neil in the Premiership. People like to watch him because he's charismatic as well as being very confrontational too.

A few months ago, Neil told me that he'd had enough of being a manager, getting soaked on the touch lines, and that the years had taken their toll. However, he hinted that there was one club that he might go to if he was offered the job, and he seemed quite optimistic about it. He wouldn't tell me the name of the club, but I hope his wish has come true!

It's sad to say, but the only other manager left in the Premier league with character and charisma is José Mourinho, who is also a brilliant coach.

The Premiership managers are so frightened about losing their jobs, that personality and jollity goes out the window.

The standard of the Premiership is second to none. Just look how it has progressed through the years. It is for sure the best league in Europe at this moment in time, which is why most of the big stars want to come here to play their football. Oh, and the money is quite good too.

I really do wish that the managers were given more time to succeed, and then we just might see a few more "Mourinhos" around. Then we would not only be wonderfully entertained by the football, but by the managers' comments too.

I remember the good old days, when clubs kept the same manager for years and years, but now the pressure is on, and if they don't get results, then they get the chop.

↖☺

Here are some of my fondest football memories, and I'm certain some of you will enjoy reading them as much as I did remembering them.

One special moment that comes to mind is the goal that John Barnes scored for England against Brazil in 1984, inside the Maracanã stadium, which was full of Brazilians screaming and shouting his name, as well as a few "Brits" who were there.

He scored a great goal, getting past five players. It's definitely a goal to be remembered forever.

I remember back in 1970, when Wolverhampton Wanderers had a brilliant, enigmatic striker called Peter Knowles (the brother of ex-Tottenham player Cyril Knowles).

Completely out of the blue, he told Wolverhampton that he was finished with football, and became a Jehovah's Witness at the ripe old age of twenty three.

He was the new George Best; he really was a special talent. Everyone at Wolverhampton was really shocked at his departure.

Knowles could do anything with a ball, and play anywhere on the field. He was almost in the full England team, and a lot of clubs were very interested in him, but sadly, he just packed his kit bag and off he went on his way.

Some of you might be a little surprised at this next memory because I have added it purely for personal reasons.

It was in 1994/95 at my beloved Hillsborough, and Sheffield Wednesday were playing against Tottenham, in their first game of the season. I had just returned to England for a short break, as I was living in Texas at the time.

Some of my old mates asked me if I would like to go to the match with them, and obviously I said yes. I was with Steve Crookes, a great old friend as well as a mad Wednesdayite; his brother Paul (alias Malcolm Macdonald lookalike); Fat (I ate all the pies) Tony from Southampton; and my brother Maurice.

It was a cracking game, with Tottenham unfortunately winning 3-4, and German Jürgen Klinsmann scoring his first goal in the Premier league with a great header.

I also remember "Hirsty" scoring a scorcher from twenty yards, a David Hirst special.

This game sticks in my head for several reasons: it was Klinsmann's debut, David Hirst's great goal, a great score-line of 3-4, and I was with a great bunch of lads. Also, it was a lovely warm opening day of the season, which can make all the difference sometimes. It was a perfect day of football (apart from Sheffield Wednesday losing!)

One story to be remembered is a match when I was playing for Sliema Wanderers in Malta. The referee had to stop the game in the first half for about ten minutes, because no one could hear him when he blew his whistle. The reason was that the RAF's Red Arrows were stationed in Malta at the time. On this particular day, the Red Arrows were practising their flying routines with about eight or nine of their jets, and the noise was horrendous. They were not only ear-splittingly loud, but they were also flying very low. We were playing an important cup game against Valetta, so the ref stopped the game until the Red Arrows had finished. How many other players can say that they had a match stopped by the Red Arrows?

⚽

One person I will always remember and miss is the legendary commentator, Ken Wolstenholme.

He had the most charismatic voice ever to grace the world of TV football commentary. To this day, I do not know of any commentator who makes my ears stand to attention like Ken could. He was brilliant at his job, with that silky, fluent voice of his, and of course, his famous one-liner at the end of the 1966 World Cup final: 'Some people are on the pitch. They think it's all over,' (then Geoff Hurst scores his third goal). 'It is now.'

That sentence is so famous that the BBC named their TV sports quiz show after it.

Ken Wolstenholme will always be remembered for that classic World Cup Final commentary, but I loved to hear his football commentaries, from the 1950s until the 1970s.

Another great memory that always puts a smile on my face is the match when Manchester City scored two goals in added time against Queens Park Rangers at the "Etihad" stadium in 2012, making them Premier League champions for the first time in the club's history.

I will never forget the sad look on the faces of the Manchester United fans. It was absolutely breath-taking, because Manchester City is my second team after Sheffield Wednesday.

I have always had an affinity with City, ever since the days of Malcolm Allison, Colin Bell and Francis Lee.

Talking of Francis Lee; I received a message from him on my mobile a couple of months ago, saying that he would call me back the following day and would hopefully arrange a meeting with me. Sadly, he never rang me back, and he hadn't left his number, and so, to this day, I'm still waiting to hear from him. I always loved watching him in his prime, and I really wanted him in my book.

Ever since the Premiership has had "total viewing" every year, there have been many great games that people remember, as well as great players too.

Every now and then, certain enigmatic players grace the Premier league, who are unforgettable for one reason or another, such as Eric Cantana (Manchester United), Jay Jay Okocha (Bolton Wanderers), Dennis Bergkamp (Arsenal), Faustino Asprilla (Newcastle United), Paolo Di Canio (Sheffield Wednesday), Paul Gascoigne (Tottenham), and how could I not mention the one and only Mario Balotelli (Manchester City).

Then there's the brilliance of Cristiano Ronaldo, Gareth Bale, Luis Suárez, and Lionel Messi, who are probably the top four best players in the world right now.

There have also been some wonderfully funny moments in the Premiership too, like Paolo Di Canio pushing the referee to the ground when playing for Sheffield Wednesday against Arsenal, and Hull City's Jimmy Bullard's team-talk at half time in the middle of the pitch, taking the p*ss out of his manager Phil Brown.

How could we ever forget "Big Ron" Atkinson's first game in charge of Nottingham Forest at home, when he sat in the wrong dugout?

Personally, my funniest moment in football was when Liverpool were playing Chelsea, and Steve Gerrard tried to shake hands with the young Chelsea mascot, but the young kid (probably only about three years old) stuck his thumb on his nose to Gerrard and also winked in the process, a very funny moment to be treasured. I've watched it over and over again!

⚽

I have also made a list of certain players who, in my opinion, excelled in certain positions, all the way back to the sixties, right up to now. Once again I will say that they are only my opinions, not everyone's, but I like to think that the majority of you will agree with me about most of them.

I will start with some of the best dribblers that I loved to watch:

David Ginola (Tottenham), Charlie Cooke (Chelsea), Eddie Gray (Leeds United), Georgi Kinkladze (Manchester City), George Best (Manchester United), and I think we can also mention another one from the past, Sir Stanley Matthews (Blackpool), a real wizard down the right wing.

Wonderful passers of the ball in my opinion include Glen Hoddle (Tottenham), Tony Currie (Sheffield United), Alan

Hudson (Chelsea), Liam Brady (Arsenal), and the brilliantly gifted Johnnie Giles (Leeds United), who had two wonderful feet.

⚽

Here are some great finishers from the past and present: George Best (Manchester United), Dennis Bergkamp (Arsenal), Alan Shearer (Newcastle United), Robbie Fowler (Liverpool), Cristiano Ronaldo (Manchester United), Jürgen Klinsmann (Tottenham), Bob Latchford (Birmingham City), Thierry Henry (Arsenal), and let's not forget the king of pouching, Jimmy Greaves (Tottenham).

⚽

There have been some wonderful headers of the ball in our top-flight English football.

I loved Ron Davies (Southampton), Duncan Ferguson (Everton), Alan Shearer (Newcastle United), and even though he was only about five feet eight inches tall, Tim Cahill (Everton) was brilliant in the air.

My all-time favourite was Alan Gilzean (Tottenham). He was magnificent to watch. He could glance it, flick it, lob it, power it, or place it anywhere he wanted. He really was the best header of a ball that I have ever seen. I honestly have never seen anyone better than him, past or present.

❦☉

Players with fire in their boots always please spectators. Every football fan wants to see a scorcher from twenty yards or so, and these following players could certainly do that.

Matt Le Tissier (Southampton), Cristiano Ronaldo (Manchester United), David Hirst (Sheffield Wednesday), Ted Phillips (Ipswich Town), and hotshot Peter Lorimer (Leeds United).

All of the above players could hit a ball with tremendous power, and Sheffield Wednesday striker, David "Hirsty" Hirst, held the record for the hardest ever shot recorded, when he hit the bar against Arsenal at a whopping 114 miles per hour, a speed only broken quite recently by Brazilian player Ronny Heberson.

❦☉

Some of the best defenders who come to mind are players like Jaap Stam (Manchester United), Colin Hendry (Blackburn Rovers), Roy McFarland (Derby County), Stuart Pearce (Nottingham Forest), John Terry (Chelsea), and the brilliant all-rounder, the mighty John Charles (Leeds United).

Most of these defenders "never took any prisoners", but they were all good solid tacklers and a very big asset to their club. Fans sometimes tend to forget about the guys at the back, just because the glamour and the glory usually comes from the strikers, because strikers score goals, and goals win games.

I think if I had to choose a defender for his hard, tenacious tackling, it would have to be Stuart Pearce, but if I was choosing a defender who had everything, including style, composure, awareness and skill, then I would pick Roy McFarland. He had everything.

In the sixties and seventies, when referees were more lenient, there were so-called "hard men" of the game, like Ron "Chopper" Harris (Chelsea), Norman "Bite your legs" Hunter (Leeds United), Roy Keane (Manchester United), Tommy Smith (Liverpool), and the dirtiest of them all, named by three ex-players in this book, Peter Storey (Arsenal).

At some stage of their careers, all the above have been shown a red card, and some of them have had more than one on a few occasions.

Some of them even had private vendettas between themselves, and other players just loved stopping opponents in any way that they could, and I do mean any!

Back in the sixties and seventies, the referees were so lenient that they would let play go on, time after time, even though players were getting kicked up and down the pitch. The kickers would get away with murder, so to speak.

These days, I am sick of seeing forwards diving in the box, week after week, trying to get a penalty, but the problem is that not only do they get the penalty sometimes, but the innocent defender gets sent off because of the stupid "last man" rule, so where do you draw the line?

The officials protect forwards a lot these days, and goal-keepers even more, so I guess we have seen the last of the "hard men".

✦❁

A player with speed always catches the eye, especially now, because the game has got so fast, it's essential to be quick.

Probably the quickest player around today in the Premiership would be Theo Walcott (Arsenal), as was Thierry Henry (Arsenal) before him.

However, the fastest of them all was able to sprint a hundred metres in 10.4 seconds. I'm talking about Malcolm Macdonald (Newcastle United). There was hardly any fat on him at all: it was pure muscle, so that he looked like he only weighed eleven stone, when in fact, he was a fourteen-stone powerhouse.

Pace is so important to the game these days, to get behind the defence, but sometimes certain people in the game are too obsessed with it. After all, Bobby Moore wasn't the quickest player, and neither was Terry Sherringham, or Matt Le Tissier, or the mighty Franz Beckenbauer.

One of my favourite wingers of all time, John Robertson of Nottingham Forest, never had any speed. He used to beat his man with skill, and subtle changes of pace. He was a defenders' nightmare when he was on song.

However, I do agree that because the game has changed so much, speed is an essential part of a player's armoury.

Colin Bell (Manchester City) had tremendous stamina; he could run forever. Even his manager at City, Malcolm Allison nicknamed him "Nijinsky", after the famous race horse, because he was so fit.

I have to say though, that the finest athlete that I have come across on a football field, not only in the Premier League but anywhere in the world, has to be Gareth Bale.

Quite honestly, the last time that I saw a player move with such grace and speed, and brilliant control too, was the late great Portuguese player Eusébio. I just love watching Bale when he's in full flight. He's so strong, and moves like a greyhound, I think he is a real treasure and it's a crying shame that he was born in Wales and not in England.

⚽

That brings me to the goal keepers now, and I have to say we've had some good ones over the years. Keepers like Peter

Schmeichel (Manchester United), Peter Shilton (Leicester City), Gordon Banks (Leicester City), and Ron Springett (Sheffield Wednesday), who by the way, was only five feet eight inches tall and played for England over thirty times. He really was a brilliant keeper in his day.

My favourite keepers of today are mostly foreign, like Petr Čech (Chelsea). He's been the best of the bunch for a few years now and he's still going strong, showing that he is still a very good capable keeper.

I have noticed how goal-keeping has changed over the years, with keepers now playing till they are forty plus, because their level of fitness is much better these days: everything is so advanced. Injuries that took three months to heal now take half the time, and like I said before, keepers are very well protected these days by the officials.

If you look at the really big clubs around the world, you will see that when a manager rebuilds a team, they usually start by acquiring a class keeper, and they don't come cheap nowadays.

Also, there have been a few lucky players in the Premiership: like Vinnie Jones (Wimbledon), who just kicked people. Robbie Savage (Birmingham City), also just kicked people, but ran about a lot more than Vinnie Jones did. I have to say that Robbie Savage always put in a full shift.

Then there's the luckiest of them all, David Beckham. No one can ever take away from him what an excellent professional he has been throughout his years as a footballer, but I have to agree with his fellow ex-England player Chris Waddle, who said that David Beckham would not get into his top thousand football players of all time.

When you take a close look at what ability Beckham had, he was basically good at passing and crossing the ball, but let's face it, any professional footballer should be able to do that.

Beckham couldn't dribble, he couldn't tackle, he couldn't head the ball, he had no pace, and being an attacking midfielder, he hardly ever scored from open play, unless it was a free kick.

I admit it, at times he's been a good leader for England, with his enthusiasm and work ethic, but on sheer skill, I cannot condone his brilliance. To be a great player, you have to actually be great, and for me David Beckham does not fit that billing.

If I was him, I would wake up every morning wondering how all this happened. I do like his demeanour in general, and he's fairly humble too, but a great England player he was not and never has been.

He has always been vastly over-rated as a player, but his fame grew when he started going out with ex-Spice girl, Victoria Adams, and the rest is history.

The only small blemish in his career happened when he was playing for Real Madrid, when there was a bit of a scandal about him messing around with his personal assistant Rebecca Loos, but it blew over quickly, probably because Loos didn't have much credence to her story. Most people think she was just looking for her fifteen minutes of fame.

He's an agent's goal mine, as you can see that he's still never off the television doing some commercial or other. Despite my grumbles, I can say that I have always liked David Beckham, and good luck to him if he can milk the football industry by using his fame, popularity, or just simply his good looks.

There is one more person that I have to mention, who played in the Premier league, and that's the Italian striker Fabrizio Ravanelli (Middlesbrough).

The only reason I have mentioned him is because my wonderful, adorable late mother thought he was the best thing since sliced bread. She was totally besotted with him, and she always loved to watch him. To be honest, he was quite a good footballer too. So, mother dear, I did mention him, because I know if I didn't, you would not be smiling down on me from above.

I have really enjoyed writing this chapter, because it was something that I could really get my teeth into.

Nonetheless, like the saying goes, "Everything has to come to an end", so I will end it by naming some players (past and present) whom I consider special for different reasons. Some because they were great characters, some because they were naturally gifted, and some because they had that certain something about them that just made you want to watch them playing football.

See how many of them that you thought were special too. I know that we all have different opinions but these are mine. Enjoy.

BRITISH PLAYERS

Ryan Giggs (Manchester United)

Gareth Bale (Tottenham)

Steven Gerrard (Liverpool)

Paul Scoles (Manchester United)

John Charles (Leeds United)

Matt Le Tissier (Southampton)

Stanley Matthews (Blackpool)

Jimmy Johnson (Celtic)

Stan Bowles (Queens Park Rangers)

Robbie Fowler (Liverpool)

Tom Finney (Preston North End)

Denis Law (Manchester United)

Jimmy Hagen (Sheffield United)

Kenny Dalglish (Liverpool)

Paul Gascoigne (Newcastle United)

Liam Brady (Arsenal)

Rodney Marsh (Queens Park Rangers)

Glenn Hoddle (Tottenham)

George Best (Manchester United)

Billy Bremner (Leeds United)

John Robertson (Nottingham Forest)

Johnnie Giles (Leeds United)

Colin Bell (Manchester City)

Jimmy Greaves (Tottenham)

OVERSEAS PLAYERS

Diego Maradona (Naples)

David Ginola (Tottenham)

Eric Cantana (Manchester United)

Michel Platini (Juventus)

Paolo Di Canio (Sheffield Wednesday)

Franco Zola (Chelsea)

Cristiano Ronaldo (Manchester United)

Gérson de Oliveira Nunes (Botafogo)

Sergio Agüero (Manchester City)

Pelé (Edson Arantes do Nascimento) (Santos)

Gerd Müller (Bayern Munich)

Eusébio da Silva Ferreira (Benfica)

Alfredo Di Stefano (Real Madrid)

Michael Laudrup (Barcelona).

Franz Beckenbauer (Bayern Munich)

Cristiano Ronaldo (Real Madrid).

Johan Cruyff (Barcelona)

Dennis Bergkamp (Arsenal)

Ferenc Puskás (Real Madrid)

Garrincha (Manuel Francisco dos Santos) (Botafogo)

Lionel Messi (Barcelona)

Thierry Henry (Arsenal)

Luis Suárez (Liverpool)

Zico (Arthur Antunes Coimbra) (Flamengo)

✿

Well, there you have it. It's been a pleasure writing and putting this book together, but I must admit it's been really hard work trying to fit it in with my daily routine, because I never stopped working.

The moment I realised that I was going to write this book, I pumped myself up and said to myself: 'give it 100%, Normy, make it interesting and funny. Get stories from the interviewees that people want to read about, as well as the facts and figures of their football achievements. So I got stuck into writing, whenever I had a spare moment.

We did have some fun, travelling up and down the motorway in every direction, taking wrong turns – on the way back from meeting Don Rogers, we almost ended up in Liverpool! I put it down to my co-driver, Steve Conroy (navigator extraordinary). Yes, of course I'm taking the p*ss!

But there were also moments to cherish, such as meeting Malcolm Macdonald in the beautiful little fishing village of Seaton Sluice near Newcastle.

I have to say that it was all a lot of fun, and a real pleasure meeting all my guests in here, and that it was definitely a worthwhile project.

I hope you have enjoyed reading the book as much as I enjoyed putting it together.

Norm Parkin.

Lightning Source UK Ltd.
Milton Keynes UK
UKOW06f1850150916

283088UK00023B/466/P

9 781326 058067